find yo
passion

second edition

find your passion

second edition

*20 tips and 20 tasks
for finding work that
makes your spirit soar*

jo parfitt

For The Old Geese

ACKNOWLEDGEMENTS

Mostly, I would like to thank Ian, my husband, for supporting me and my determination to work with passion. And my parents, who were always thrilled with my achievements, whatever they were. And to my boys, Sam and Josh, who know how important my work is to me and knock before they enter my office. They also get involved with my work whenever they can, for which I am both grateful and flattered.

But I also need to thank Jacinta Noonan, who helped me devise and run the first Find Your Passion workshop in November 2004. Jacinta with a little help from Fiona Cowan and Nancy Mayer, have helped me to learn to sing again. Thanks too to Rebecca Law, my onetime prodigy, who continues to convince me that I am on the right track and who helped with the case studies in this second edition.

Thanks too, to Trish Tucker, who runs Passion 4 Juice, and who has contributed her thoughts on the importance of passion to this book.

Finally, thanks to all those people: clients, students, friends, who have told me I made a difference to their lives. Without your feedback, I would never have dared to believe that I was on the right track.

FOREWORD

If you're looking for passion, you've certainly come to the right place. Jo Parfitt's passion overflows on these pages of her newly-updated book and it can't help but rub off on you, so be warned.

In the movie *Adapation*, Meryl Streep's character confessed "I do have one unembarrassed passion. I want to know what it feels like to care about something passionately."

Jo genuinely encourages our internal 'Meryl Streep' to rethink what is important to us, what drives us and where we would really love to be. She combines her advice, strategies and personal anecdotes with hands-on exercises to encourage us to both dream big and to commit to an ongoing action plan for improving our lives and filling them with passion.

Since Jill and I started developing ExpatWomen.com in March 2006, hundreds of people have written to us and told us how they needed to reinvent their lives, careers and identities when they moved overseas. I praise Jo's wisdom in referring to these crossroads in our lives as a unique opportunity to find out where our true passions lie, rather than dwelling on the who/what/where we used to be.

From personal experience, I completely agree with Jo that finding your passion can transform your life and I wish all of you the same personal satisfaction and fulfilment. Until then... as Jo says... "Time flies when you're having fun" – so soak up every experience like a sponge and be ready when your passion train leaves the station – because it could be the ride of your life.

Andrea Martins

Andrea Martins is the Co-Founder of ExpatWomen.com - a website designed to help all expatriate women living outside of their home country. Andrea and her website partner, Jill Lengré, followed their passion of helping women succeed in new locations by creating a website that is well on track to quickly becoming the #1 website for Expatriate Women worldwide.

WHY I WROTE THIS BOOK

When I was nine I knew what I wanted to be when I grew up. I wanted to be a singer. But when I was only picked for the school choir as a last resort to make up numbers, I began to believe I could not sing.

When I was fifteen I knew what I wanted to be when I grew up. I wanted to be a writer. But my school careers adviser told me that writing was not a proper career and that I should do French because that was what I was best at. So I did.

I loved acting, but, when I won five cups in a row in a drama competition and my school friends laughed at the photograph of me in the local paper, I gave up my drama lessons. At 17 I was in the national quarter finals of a public speaking competition, giving what was supposed to be an unscripted speech. I learned my lines, got flustered and forgot them. Panicked, started again and made a fool of myself. I have been petrified of learning lines ever since.

But my passion for words proved greater than I thought and was determined to win through at any cost. I did my French degree, and while I was spending my year in France, came up with the title for a cookery book: *French Tarts*. It was accepted by the first publisher I approached – I had never cooked anything in my life before – but I was passionate about food and France and writing. I learned then, aged 24, that if I was passionate about what I wanted to do, I could succeed at anything.

As for the singing, well, that has only just dared to re-emerge and though the thought of doing karaoke terrifies me, I have been taking singing lessons for a year.

I've never dared join an amateur dramatic group but I have come to love public speaking, only never with a script. Put me on a stage with an audience and I am in my element.

But you know, I'm in my 40's now, and have a husband and two great children. I love what I do for a living, but if you gave me the choice between seeing my sons in the school play, or going to Dubai to run a writing course with all expenses paid, I'd pick the play. I realise I am passionate about lots of things: about my family, friends, travel, nature, art, the theatre and cooking and sharing food.

I wrote this book because I believe that if you are to live a balanced, happy life, you have to put some passion into as many areas of it as you can. So, maybe you can indulge your passion for music at the weekend, your passion for mathematics in your day job and your love of nature during your holidays. If you love scuba-diving, you might not be able to scuba-dive for a living, or do it every day, but you can read about it, watch films about it and take a holiday near a coral reef now and again.

As illustrated earlier, with my own story, we lose sight of our passions over time. Sometimes it's through peer pressure, sometimes it's because we take bad advice and sometimes it's because we get too busy and other things get in the way. This book is to help you dig out the passions you used to have, uncover the ones you have now, if only you had the time to think about them, and to work on a blueprint for success.

Jo Parfitt

MY MISSION

Back in 1999, I attended a workshop entitled 'Write Your Own Mission Statement'. It was run by Dane, Helen Eriksen (www.going-beyond.dk), and held at the Women's International Networking (WIN) conference (www.winconference.com), in Milan. At the end of the workshop Helen encouraged us to write a one-sentence mission statement that was based on our values. I remember mine was: 'Using my talents to share what I know, inspire and support others'. Today, this has evolved into the snappier 'share what I know to help others to grow'.

Since then, this has remained my mission. I am a writer, an author, a publisher, a book cook, (www.thebookcooks.com) a speaker and a teacher. All these media allow me to share, inspire and support others. This book is just one of the ways I am able to fulfil my dreams.

I remember, many years ago, that a friend told me that my business card should simply say 'Personal Inspirer'. That is what I do best. I inspire and motivate others to make change in their lives. You can join in the fun by signing up to my newsletter, The Inspirer, or looking at my blogs via my websites.

My mission is to inspire you to be the person you were born to be, to find your truth and to live and work with passion, so that when you 'walk your talk' you are tall, proud and full of energy.

My mission is to give people the wings with which they can fly alone.

CONTENTS

INTRODUCTION

HOW I FOUND MY PASSIONS

I firmly believe you can do what you love and earn money from it. I've always believed this – despite the day at school when my careers advisor informed me, at age 14, that writing was not a career option but just an indulgence! That was when I began my attempts at conforming. And though I had written my first poem at six, my first play at 13, kept a diary since age 11 and penned hundreds of letters, I still shelved my dream.

I loved French though. And for me that included the literature, the language, the people, the country and even the teacher (not literally, I add, but Mr Feather certainly turned me into a francophile). This was also the subject in which I received the best marks. So I went to university to study French. I knew I didn't want to be a teacher, nor a translator, which seemed to be the only options open to me at the time, but I loved the language and that was enough. Somehow, deep down, I realised that French alone was not going to keep me fulfilled forever. I needed to be creative, and so it was during the year spent in France, teaching English conversation to a group of despondent teenagers, that I found the perfect outlet. I would write a book called *French Tarts*.

The title came to me in a flash one day as I walked aimlessly past one of the town's *patisseries* and immediately I knew it would happen. Not once did it strike me that I couldn't cook. I knew I had a great idea and a great title, and that my pursuit of authentic recipes from real French people would get me a few invitations to dinner. Food too is a major passion of mine.

It's funny, but you know, when you do something based on your passions it shows. Not only did I believe in my idea but I managed to convey my enthusiasm to a publisher; despite the fact that I did not even own an oven in the dingy flat in which I lived above the boiler room at College Albert Schweizer nor had I cooked any of the recipes myself. I had, however, studied every French recipe book on which I could lay my hands, and sampled more tarts than I would like to admit. I had also read widely about Normandy's local produce and felt I had the authority to discuss the benefit of putting fresh cream into pastry. I guess, what I had been doing inadvertently, yet naturally, was putting my passion to good use and become a bit of an expert in my subject. Only I did not realise that at the time.

Anyway, my plan worked. Octopus, the first publisher whom I approached with my idea, snapped it up. I quickly taught myself to type and use a word processor so that I could produce the manuscript. My first book came out in English in 1985 and then in France, in French, the following year. What's more, it appeared in an exhibition at the Pompidou Centre in Paris, as an example of one of the finest cookery books of the year. At the time, I put this immense good fortune down to beginner's luck. I had become a writer after all. I was 24 years old. I was doing something I loved and earning money. Since then, I have refused to do anything if I do not enjoy it. What happened next was a surprise, even to me.

I tried hard to come up with more cookery book ideas, found myself an agent and pitched like crazy. The doors were closed. Instead of finding more work as a cookery writer, I found myself teaching word processing – the skill I'd only learned in order to produce the manuscript for *French Tarts*. This happened mostly by accident.

Having gone to London to seek my fortune I had decided that I would like to learn to manage a restaurant and found myself a trainee management position in a large chain of wine bars. It lasted six weeks. Once I had discovered that there was no room for creativity in that kitchen and that as a manager I was responsible for decisions and administration not dreaming up menus, I quit. But I had loved working with people and dealing with clients, which led me to consider a career in recruitment. In the end I landed up in an agency that specialised in word processing.

Fortunately, I was not daunted by the prospect of learning and teaching new programs. In fact, I soon found that writing training courses left lots of room for creativity and that I loved teaching. I also liked producing the documentation and course handouts, so there I was writing again. Along the way, I was coming to learn that I loved teaching very much indeed.

The work energised me. I would never have dreamed that my creative soul would enjoy something as technical as word processing – but it did. I found that I enjoyed the lessons, meeting new people and watching the students learn and grow. In my own small way I was changing people's lives for the better. My enthusiasm must have showed because one of my clients asked me to go and work for him, developing some new computer training materials. The idea excited me and so, aged 25, I went freelance as a writer and teacher and have never looked back. From the moment I conceived the idea of French Tarts to the day I took a leap of faith and decided to run a business based on my passion had taken three years.

Two years later, I had written ten computer handbooks in plain language for some of England's largest publishers and was running a thriving computer-training and writing company.

Then I moved abroad.

LIFE WITHOUT WORK

When I arrived in Dubai the day after my wedding to Ian, who was already based there working for a large oilfield services company, they put a stamp in my passport that read 'not permitted to take up employment'. I was devastated. I had a few writing contracts to complete that I'd brought with me, but would have to spend six weeks waiting for my computer to arrive so I could begin work. Until that moment my work had been my life and my passion. I'd developed few other interests and knew no one in Dubai. With no company support, I had no idea where to look for friends or things to do. Work was all I knew. By then, ironically, I had become quite a good cook, but knew no one to invite round for dinner. If I were to count my list of passions on my fingers they would have been writing, teaching, cooking and being with people. I was in desperate need of an outlet.

Two days before my computer arrived, Ian came home from the office to find me crouched on the floor of our beautiful apartment, ripping a newspaper to shreds and crying my eyes out from sheer frustration. Without work I was a fish out of water.

Of course I could have attended Arabic language classes, or learned to paint in watercolours. I could have joined the gym, or asked my husband to introduce me to the wives of his colleagues and friends so that I could meet them for coffee in one of the many plush malls that mushroomed over there. I could have taken advantage of the wonderful swimming pool and tennis courts that went with our apartment. I could have taken a taxi and explored the city. But all I wanted to do was work, and nothing else would do.

I had lost my professional identity. My personal identity too was so intertwined with work that I had forgotten who I was without it. I had no idea that volunteer work or taking classes might have fulfilled me (today it is a different story). My mission was to find a way to use my passions and feel like myself again. Being beholden to my husband and his company made me feel impotent, invisible. We had maid service in the apartment, so I had little to do. Shorts and tee-shirts didn't need much ironing. Despite the fact that I soon had a driving licence, I was nervous about taking to the roads alone. I felt like a hollow woman. I didn't feel whole without my computer and some work to do.

It pleased me to have a label. I was a 'writer' and a 'computer trainer'. I was not 'just a wife' and the very idea made me feel hugely uncomfortable. I realised I had a personal need, not only to have a professional identity, but also to earn my own money – however little. I didn't want to have to ask my husband for the money with which to buy his birthday present.

I appreciate that my own case may be extreme, and over the years I have mellowed enormously and even taken up a few hobbies – but I am sure I'm not unique. In the 19 years since this time I have spoken with countless others in my position and learned that women often feel lost as I did when they are going through a transition. Recognising what you love to do and then prioritising putting it into practise as soon as you can in a new environment is key. But it is not just women who feel like this. I believe that we all reach a crossroads in our lives and wonder who we are and what makes us tick. For many, this happens in our mid thirties or forties, but the thunderbolt attacks us just the same.

HOW I PUT PASSION INTO MY LIFE

Well, my computer did arrive and I completed the five remaining book contracts I had taken with me. But once they had finished, I soon learned that editors found it difficult to liaise with overseas authors. This was before we had email and fax machines. Moreover, while I had started out at a time when there were many different word processing programs (MultiMate, WordPlex, DisplayWrite and all those WordStars), a new word-processing program had come to be and now everyone was using it. Word. My market dried up. Reluctantly, with no more book-writing in the pipeline, I realised I had to go back to the drawing board and create another new career for myself.

Ian had promised me that we would only be abroad for six months or so – but the thought of even a few months' sabbatical filled me with horror. I simply had to look for alternative employment.

Despite the stamp in my passport that apparently didn't allow me to work, I discovered that not all hope was lost. In fact, working in Dubai was remarkably easy. Providing you found a local company to sponsor you and supply a labour card, you could do almost anything at all.

It is all a question of looking out for opportunities and listening to what people tell you they need. The first thing someone told me they needed was a CV. My ears pricked up at once. I had worked in a recruitment agency so knew what a CV needed to look like and my computing experience meant that I had no problem making it look pretty. And, I could write and interview. I had an idea. Maybe the recruitment agencies in Dubai would like to offer a CV writing service? I asked one, and they agreed. Before long, I decided to ask them if they would like a computer-training department too. They agreed to that too and in one fell swoop I had a labour card and a job to go to. I was writing. I was teaching. I was with people. I was happy.

But times change and opportunities come and go, as did my job at the agency. Yet as each door closed I could already see a new one opening and I grabbed the chance to find another way to utilise my passion. As long as I could write or teach, or be with people I'd be OK.

Over the next six years in Dubai, three in Oman and two in Norway, I developed a range of complementary and changing careers that I dipped into when the opportunity arose. I was also happy to discard some career streams when the market disappeared. This ability to reinvent myself and be flexible has been key to my success. Each reinvention has taken place because I first looked inside myself to see which skills, interests and passions most excited me at that time.

Always keen to learn new things there were times when I acquired new passions, times when I let some slide for a while, and times when I was determined to combine some, like writing and teaching, for example, or writing and cooking, or French and teaching. Since I had been a child, I had always loved to be on a stage, and while I no longer chose to do any acting as the rehearsal schedule no longer fit my lifestyle as a mother, being a teacher and speaker filled that need.

If I look inside myself today, I see the following key skills, all of which have grown out of my passions:

- Creativity
- Writing

- Teaching
- Helping people to grow
- Flexibility
- Willingness to learn
- Desire for variety
- Love of people
- Communication
- Computer skills
- French
- Cooking
- Connecting people through informal networking
- Books – reading and writing
- Entrepreneurship
- Making things happen

These core skills have led me to become a journalist, a teacher of writing, a teacher of French conversation, a copywriter, a publisher of a date cookery book, a copy typist, a curriculum vitae producer, a computer teacher, a trainer of trainers, a computer training centre course developer, a Dorling Kindersley book distributor, a manufacturer and marketer of date chutney, the organiser of a take-away curry service (my Indian nanny and housekeeper in Oman was a fabulous cook), a founder of writers' circles and professional women's networks, a speaker, a workshop presenter, editor, newsletter producer and of course author and publishing consultant.

Of course, not all of my pursuits have been a roaring success. In fact, some have bombed! Only last year I had a great idea for a birthday calendar that featured amusing photographs with funny captions that would appeal to expats in the Netherlands. One showed a field of tulips, only the flowers had been replaced with balls of a famous local red cheese. The caption read 'Garden of Edam'. Sure, it was a good idea and the calendars looked wonderful because I hired a professional photographer. But though I was passionate about my idea and loved my jokes, I am less enthusiastic about going round local retailers trying to sell them products. In one year, I sold 70 copies. Fortunately, I only printed 100.

The Dorling Kindersley book sales job was wonderful at first. I love books, and in Oman at the time, it was hard to get decent books in English and DK were well known for their fabulous publications. I held parties in people's homes and everyone loved the products so I sold hundreds every time. Only, I am less passionate about research and bureaucracy than I am about books and going to parties and discovered after just a few months that my business was not exactly legal so was forced to give up.

Likewise some of my ventures have been more lucrative than others, but the enjoyment I derived from doing them made me consider them to be worthwhile. The take-away service for example, was not legal either, and really just involved me telling all my friends about Julie's cooking, producing a price list and taking the orders for her. I made no money from this, and never intended to, but it was a lot of fun. Neither did I make any money directly from running the writers' circles and women's networks. However, by being the figurehead of a group meant that lots of people came to know who I was and would pass me referrals. Many of those who attended the free writers' circles would end up asking me to run a course for them too.

Sometimes we need to consider doing some things purely because we are passionate about them, and enjoy them enormously, rather than for the money. I have found that when we do something we love our enthusiasm is so evident that this results in many unexpected opportunities. The voluntary work I did for the Shell Outpost Family Archive Centre, helping them to research and publish a book, meant that I was later offered a paid part-time position at the centre as its co-director.

In addition, you may find yourself with a lifestyle that does not allow you to employ your greatest passions in paid work. This is the time when you should try to find voluntary work, study opportunities or hobbies that would allow you that outlet instead. So, for example, when I discovered that there was less need for a journalist in Oman than in Dubai, I decided it was time to take a short story writing course instead. I was driven to devote part of my time to writing, that I was not being paid for it was not so important at the time.

If I look inside myself, I can also see the values that motivate me and make my professional life work for me. Some people value money, others value fame, free time, flexible hours or variety. Values change over time and it's worth taking a look at yours regularly. If you want to be true to yourself, you need to consider your values as well as your passions. My values, right now, are:

- Sharing
- Supporting others
- Making a difference
- Using my passions
- Interacting with people
- Being accessible and affordable
- Keeping a balance of working alone and with others
- Making time for myself and my family
- Developing a specialism
- Being authentic

While you consider your values you might like to think about how your ideal life might look. Would you work three days a week? Would you work part-time? In term time only? Or would you, like many expatriates, want such a flexible schedule that you could take advantage of more trips away than normal, and to have enough time when visitors came to stay?

When we lived in Dubai and Oman, like many, I had help in the house, so I had more time at my disposal. However, once the baking hot days of summer came, I wanted to return to Europe with our small children for six weeks or more. Not many 'on the economy' positions would make this possible. My freelance life did.

Now we are in the Netherlands and the children are teenagers, I no longer feel the need to be home for them all day in the school holidays or directly after school. As a result I have more time on my hands in which to work. However, now that the children are older, I am not involved in play dates and school runs, and so have no chance to meet other people unless I make the effort to go out to work or to get involved with other people.

As we move through the different ages and stages of life our needs change and with them our values and our passions. While, for me, writing and teaching have been core to my being for more than 20 years now, other passions become more necessary, with my love of being with people increasing as my children needed me less at home.

Reading the last few pages, I expect that some of you will have recognised some of your own values and passions in mine. Others will be no closer to identifying what they most love to do. I find that the more we get involved in life and the more responsibilities and commitments we take on, the less chance we have to be introspective. The older we get and the longer we leave looking inside ourselves to rediscover and name our passions, the harder it gets and the longer ago it seems that we last *knew* who we were. That's why I wrote this book. You will find the 20 tips and 20 tasks that follow will inspire you to get to know yourself better. It is filled with tricks that have helped me and countless others, I never stop learning and finding new ways to identify my passions.

You see, finding your passion is just the first step. The next step is to *do* something about it and to find a way to fit it into your life.

Making things happen should be the step you pledge to take once you have found your passions. Most of the time I have been determined to put my passions into my work. Paid work. So, having examined my passions and my values, needs and wants at the time, I would look carefully at the local market, to see where the gaps lay, or where I might have found the most luck in finding an outlet for one or more of my passions. Then, I would network like mad and ask lots of questions (sadly, in Oman, I forgot to talk to any lawyers!) until I had formed a plan of action. Once I had a plan I would take a deep breath and start taking steps towards making it happen. And, you know, sometimes that first step was not so hard.

But sometimes, things are really tough. I have lived abroad as part of an expatriate household for 14 of the 21 years that I have been freelance. Abroad, we have been lucky enough not to need me to produce a solid second income. This was a terrific opportunity and gave me permission to do only what I most enjoyed. But when your family needs a second income, as ours did on repatriation to the UK a few years ago for a stint of seven years, your dreams may take a little honing.

MAINTAINING A PASSION-BASED CAREER WHEN YOU NEED THE MONEY!

When we repatriated in 1997 I had to earn some money. The first project I worked on when we came home was the publication of *A Career in Your Suitcase*. I formed Summertime Publishing and, during 1998, launched this title and another called *Forced To Fly*. This took a lot of work and investment, and the returns were relatively small at first – so I decided to develop a range of seminars and workshops on the theme of portable careers. I soon discovered that, on average, about a quarter of delegates would buy a book too. And while these seminars were successful and well received, the marketing response was slow to start with. Along the way I discovered that those who most wanted me to speak, and whom I most loved addressing, tended to be non-profit associations and international conferences – who had little, if any, budget. If I was to meet my financial target I had to think again.

Once more I looked inside myself, and decided that I had to calculate which among my many careers had the most earning potential. I had to think hard about which of my skills would earn me the most money per hour and for which there was also a market. During my soul searching I realised it was time to take my journalism to UK based magazines and newspapers.

I love writing, as you know, and find it easy, though in order to give me the most satisfaction I needed to write about subjects that interested me. It became clear that I had picked up a few more skills and passions to add to my list. I could now call myself an expert on expatriate living and portable careers and began in earnest to look for opportunities. Within a few months I was writing for

Resident Abroad (later called *FT Expat*), *The Weekly Telegraph*, *Women's Business Magazine* and the *Smart Moves* section of *The Independent on Sunday*.

During this period, when I had to contribute 50 per cent of our family budget, journalism became my job. Portable career presentations and publishing were my career. Both were based on my passions but one became less of a pleasure when I was forced to do it day after day. At that time I could earn what I needed by writing eight articles a month in addition to my other work. That meant that I had not only to *write* them but to *sell* them too. And though I am good at selling it is a skill I have developed rather than one I am passionate about. At first my job funded my career – but over time the two merged until I was able to pick and choose my writing projects and my presenting started to earn me money.

When, in 2000, three years later, I was offered the chance to edit a new magazine, called *Woman Abroad*, I didn't hesitate to accept. Without a doubt, this position was the culmination of my career experiences and it allowed me to exercise all my skills and values at once. I was flying. Being on the payroll, albeit as a freelance for three days a week, meant that I did not have to keep selling my writing, though I could write as much as I wanted. This job had the added benefit of being able to commission other writers. I am passionate about growing new writers, empowering and helping them to forge a new career and so this gave me the chance to develop newcomers. That was best of all.

But a couple of years later, *Woman Abroad* closed. People loved the magazine, but the aftermath of the 9/11 bombings left our advertisers and subscribers unsure whether life abroad had a future. And, for me, I had to go back to the drawing board.

I am a firm believer in the fact that if you are on course and doing what you are meant to do in life you get great feedback. For years I had been helping people to write their books. I had edited a few, appraised a few manuscripts and given lots of advice. Maybe this was what I needed to do next? I took a leap of faith.

The next time someone asked me what I did for a living I would answer with the words 'I help people to write their books'. At a networking event the following week, someone did ask me and so I took a deep breath and answered with my new words.

'That's terrific,' he said. 'Can you help me?'

And so my newest career began. That was in 2002 and since then I have rebranded myself as a Book Cook. This image provides the perfect combination of my skills and passions. I love to cook as you know, and have written two cookery books. I also realised many years ago that writing a book and cooking had much in common. They both need a recipe, or formula, and the right ingredients and method too. Since I became The Book Cook, I have helped many clients to make their publishing dreams come true. Things have become so busy that I now have a team of other Book Cooks working with me, and we have clients all over the world and offer a complete service from pipedream, through publishing to profit and PR.

Today my main career focuses on writing and helping others to get published. The more I learn about the subject the more I have to share. This is why I am constantly developing workshops and running them all over the world on all aspects of writing and publishing. I never stop learning, never stop finding new things to be passionate about, and then, in turn, sharing that knowledge.

MY PASSION FILTER

In 2005 we moved again, to the Netherlands this time. Again, I had to start again and establish my business in a new country. Two years on, I can proudly say that the move has added to my career, not taken away. The Book Cooks team has grown to include Sous Chefs in the Netherlands as well as in the USA and UK.

Now, I can safely say that a move does not daunt me as much as it once did. I know exactly what my passions are and what I need to achieve in order to live and work authentically in any location. My passions have become portable and thanks to my belief in networking, volunteering and that my role is to share what I know to help others to grow, I can get up and running fast. Each time a new opportunity comes my way I run the idea through my Passion Filter to check whether it might be worth pursuing. Here are my rules:

- Does it allow me to still be available for my family and friends?
- Does it feed my soul?
- Does it feel good, deep in my gut?
- Would I want to do this day after day?
- Does it excite me?
- Does it fit in with at least one of my passions?
- Does it allow me to be authentic?
- Does it energise me?
- Does it earn me an appropriate amount of money/pleasure/learning in exchange for the investment of my time?
- Does it let me be a free spirit?
- Is it flexible enough?
- Is it creative enough?
- Does it let me learn new things?

- Does it allow me to 'be' rather than 'do'?
- Does it fit with my mission statement of 'Sharing what I know to help others to grow.'

I believe it's my right to be able to do what I love for a living. If I want to be energised by my work, to look forward to each morning, to be authentic and enthusiastic, then it is vital that I'm passionate about my work. If we do what we love then our enthusiasm and energy will do our marketing for us.

If you are passionate about something it shows in your body language, your words, your facial expressions. Then, if you have it right, you convince other people that you care about what you do and they believe in you. When people believe that you are passionate about what you do they will tell others about you and give you referrals. More than 15 years ago I read a book by Marsha Sinetar, called *Do What You Love The Money Follows*. It's true.

FIRST, FIND YOUR ROLE MODEL

For this second edition of *Find Your Passion* I took a look at my own life and considered what helped me to find my passion and have the confidence to go out there and actually start a business based on what I loved to do. We all need role models and mentors, and you can explore this area yourself in Tip Seventeen, and many of us may have just the inspiration we need on our own doorstep. My father was a fine role model to me. He spent 30 years teaching in a technical college and though he loved the teaching and the holidays he hated the bureaucracy and the politics and was always grumbling about it.

He, like me (he is frighteningly like me), had always loved to write and then, aged 55, when I was at university and my younger brother still at home, he took early retirement and became a freelance author. Many people of his age, with family and financial commitments, would not have taken such a step, but I watched my father get up in the morning with a smile on his face and go out to write in a tiny attic room he had rented in town. If he could dare to make a living out of writing at 55, then what was stopping me at 25, when I had no financial commitments?

The eleven case studies you can read at the end of this book have all been written by real people, just like you and me, with or without commitments, who have decided to make their dream a reality. Mike Chissick was newly widowed with two young children when he changed career. Jim Wheat newly married and living in Dubai, a place where there is no National Health Service and accommodation is expensive, took a leap into the unknown by starting his own business. Diana Store was living in accommodation that was one step up from a squat when she started her raw food business, and Pat Reeves terminally ill when she began FoodAlive. When Kate Atkin decided to leave the safe world of banking and go it alone in a completely new field, her first safe contract did not materialise but still she stood firm and believed in herself and the viability of her business.

If you do what you love then you will find the motivation to make it happen. You will find a way of overcoming obstacles. Your passion will show on your face and your enthusiasm will make others believe in you, invest in you and pass you referrals. When you work with passion you become not only your brand, but your best advert.

If you choose to run a business based on your passions then you have much better chance of success than if you run a business that pays well but does not quite 'float your boat'. After all, you are the one who will have to get up in the morning for 48 weeks a year, maybe more. Isn't it important that you spend the majority of your waking life doing something that you love? But the first step is to find out what on earth it is that you truly love to do. This book will show you how.

Enjoy the journey

Jo Parfitt, Den Haag, 2007

TIPS AND TASKS

TIP ONE – BELIEVE IN BLUE SKY

A few years ago I chose myself a new motto. I chose the words 'believe in blue sky' and it has stuck. I chose it for several reasons.

When I was living in Norway it rained all the time. Or at least it seemed to. For an entire year there was never a day I left the house without my raincoat. And when it rained, it rained! Horizontal sheets of rain would soak me through. Everyone wore rain trousers. And then I met an American called Kit Prendergast. One day Kit turned up on my doorstep, dripping wet. Her hair was plastered to her face and there was a large drip on the end of her nose. Yet Kit stood on my doorstep and grinned from ear to ear.

'Proactive people take their weather with them,' she said. And I knew just what she meant. In fact the Norwegians have a saying of their own, which is: 'There is no such thing as bad weather – just bad clothes.' Both Kit and the Norwegians are right. If you stay optimistic it does not matter what the weather is like.

The Brits too are concerned with the weather. We constantly peer up at the grey, cloud filled sky in search of a piece of blue big enough to patch a sailor's trousers. We see so little sunshine yet we stand firm in our belief that 'it is brightening up' and that we can see scraps of blue sky out there among the clouds.

The Americans, however, use the term 'to blue sky' to mean that they brainstorm and think laterally about all the good things they could do and the best ways to tackle problems. If they get together to 'blue sky' they will not be talking of negatives but of all the best outcomes, dreams coming true and what they would do if money were no object.

So, you see, when I say believe in blue sky I mean that we should:

- Stay positive
- Be proactive
- Talk about our dreams
- Share our dreams with other people
- Allow other people to join us and inspire us to make our dreams come true
- Believe that, despite the clouds, blue sky is just around the corner

TASK ONE

One of the best ways to kick-start the search deep into your soul and into your past for your long lost passions, is to have a Blue Sky Party. Get some friends together for a relaxed and informal evening and tell them that they have to come armed with their dreams, hopes and open minds. Then, if say, you invite seven friends over for two hours, that means that everyone gets 15 minutes each in the limelight.

Friends are likely to be honest with you, to tell you what they think you are passionate about and to tell you, frankly, where they think you are lousy. So go on, plan your Blue Sky Party today.

Name seven people you would like to invite to your party (with you that makes eight in total)

1

2

3

4

5

6

7

Write some notes about how you will cater for them. Passionfruit punch, passion cake and passionfruit cocktails maybe? A cake decorated with white icing and patches of blue sky and blue curacao cocktails? How about your favourite food? Or you could ask everyone to bring along their favourite dish. You could even decorate the table with passion flowers.

23

_____

_____

_____

Just a little effort will go a long way and help your guests to really enjoy themselves and loosen up their memories. Perhaps you could make all your guests wear blue? What else might you do?

_____

_____

_____

OK, there's nothing left for it but to name the date and time of your party:

Date: _____

Time: _____

At the end of your party make sure that everyone promises to do at least one thing to feed their passion within the following week. Set a date to meet again and find out how you all got on.

TIP TWO – WHAT MATTERS?

Do you know what matters to you? What could you do that would make you instantly spring into action and put an associated task right to the top of your to do list?

When you hear that there is a half price cashmere sale are you down there like a shot? Maybe shopping for bargains is your passion?

When you hear that a friend is ill do you dash round there to offer a shoulder to cry on and to help with the children or the shopping? Maybe caring for others is your passion?

Do you find yourself getting hot under the collar when people are talking about politics, the chopping down of rainforests, famine or ecology? Maybe you are passionate about making a difference in these areas?

Is your family one of the most important things to you in the world? Your home, your garden, your friends, your work or maybe even your time off?

If something matters to you then it is important that you allow yourself to say so and to do something about it. For example, if eating organic food matters to you, then you would always choose to buy organic produce, rather than processed alternatives. If you are passionate about the theatre, you need to give yourself the chance to go to the theatre once in a while, join an amateur dramatic group, set up a play reading circle or subscribe to a theatre magazine. You can only be authentic and true to yourself and others if you walk your talk. Bearing grudges or whining 'if only' is not very productive, is it? Moreover, living falsely can cause unnecessary stress.

The things that matter to you are often called your *values*.

Sometimes it can be really hard to know what we value. We can be so busy earning money, doing the shopping, ensuring games kit is washed and ready and that the children have not been left abandoned at the school gates, that we rarely stop to think about what we value most.

Funnily enough, according to surveys, most people put well-being at the top of their list of what matters. Yet too few of us do anything about it. Do you exercise regularly? Eat natural foods and keep your brain and body healthy?

So, here are some examples to help you work out what may matter to you:

- If an opportunity arose out of the blue to go to a conference, a concert, a flower show or an impromptu class concert at the school, would you move mountains to get there?

- What do you read? Is there any topic that would make you buy a newspaper, watch a television programme or buy a book on that subject?

- When you are out with friends, what topics of conversation have you sitting up in your seat, desperate to join in?

TASK TWO

Write down six things that you know, instinctively matter to you:

1

2

3

4

5

6

Just in case you still feel stuck and can't really work out what you value, here is a list of possible values to choose from to jog your memory. Take a highlighter pen and mark all those that ring true for you. Promise yourself that you will think about putting some of these values into your life, starting today.

- Administering
- Advising
- Being authentic
- Being different
- Challenge
- Communicating
- Counselling
- Creativity
- Dealing with details
- Environmental issues
- Family
- Flexibility
- Helping
- Inspiring
- International environment
- Leading

- Learning
- Listening
- Making a change
- Making a difference
- Making money
- Moving
- Nature
- Organising
- Responsibility
- Sharing
- Solving problems
- Supporting others
- Taking time off
- Teamwork
- Travel
- Variety
- Working alone
- Working from home
- Working with animals
- Working with numbers

Now pick your four top choices from the list and chart above. Select four things you know, that if you had to sacrifice all the others, you could never live without.

Write them here:

1

2

3

4

Now write down when, in the next month you will make time for those values.

1

2

3

4

Now transfer these items directly to your diary!

TIP THREE - YOUR LABEL IS SHOWING

If you are to live your life authentically, and with time for your passions, you need to portray on the outside the way you are on the inside. Then, with your 'passion on your sleeve' so to speak, you will find that more opportunities will appear that allow you to be yourself and to work with passion. The right people will be drawn to you and you can live the life you want.

We all have an idea of how we appear to others and how this may differ from how we see ourselves. It can be very revealing when we also take a look at how we view others.

First impressions can be a dangerous thing. Only last week I sat with complete strangers over lunch at a local fund raising event. A lady sat opposite me and all I saw was the fact that she seemed to have a hunched back and that her hair was so unnaturally thick and dark that it had to be a wig. Immediately I branded her as a weirdo and a fuddyduddy. But later, during coffee, she started a conversation with me. She was lively and intelligent and we found that we both shared a passion for French literature. A little later she attended a workshop with me and I watched her as she almost danced into the room, she was so light on her feet. During the workshop she was the life and soul of the party. I bet that lady thought her outward appearance showed people her true personality, sadly, it didn't.

And I have had a similar, humiliating experience myself. Once, when I attended a workshop, led by Gail MacIndoe, on making things happen, we were all told to turn to the person on our left and tell them honestly what our first impressions of them had been that day. My neighbour told me that I looked friendly and accessible (phew!) but that my brown suit made me look dull and boring. Then, two years later, when I was telling this story to fellow diners at the Global Living conference, Huw turned to me, and said 'I know that suit, you wore it at the Women on the Move conference in 1998, didn't you? You looked terrified and she was right, the suit was terrible!' That someone had remembered seeing that suit four years earlier was bad enough, but a man noticing, made it ten times worse!

That suit soon went to the charity shop and I learned a tough lesson. It is said that people form an impression of someone within the first few seconds of meeting. I realised that I only had a few seconds to look the part: dynamic, exciting, inspiring, fun and of course, friendly and accessible.

So, I went to see a style and image consultant and discovered which colours, shapes and styles were right for my colouring and personality. And once I knew that I began to dress like, a 'Classic, Romantic, Spring' and felt that at least I would get noticed for the right reasons. But a couple of years later, I felt that while much that was Classic, Romantic Spring, was appropriate it did not allow me to wear the Omani silver Bedouin jewellery I adored and had collected when we lived in Muscat. Furthermore, as a creative, I wanted to find a way of putting my personality into my wardrobe. This time I called on Sue Donnelly (www.accentuate.me.uk), author of several Bookshaker (www.bookshaker.com) publications who helped me to see that it was OK to break a few rules as long as I did it properly. My passion now lives happily in my growing wardrobe.

TASK THREE

Write down four words describing how you think you look, sound and behave when you are at work.

1

2

3

4

Write down four words describing how you think you look, sound and behave when you are not at work, say, at the weekend, or on holiday.

1

2

3

4

Now ask your friends how they think you look, sound and behave. Write those words down here:

1

2

3

4

Now ask your colleagues or clients how they think you look, sound and behave. Write those words down here:

1

2

3

4

Now find someone who hardly knows you at all, preferably someone you have never even spoken to, and ask them about their first impressions of you. Make them promise to be honest.

1

2

3

4

What could you do, right now, to help yourself to portray the right image?

TIP FOUR - YOUR UNIQUE CONTRIBUTION

Every day, millions of people get up and go to work to do a job that they do not much like, but that pays the bills. Many people no longer work to live, they live to work. Work is all-consuming. It takes up evenings, weekends and now, thanks to mobile phones and wireless Internet, people even work on holiday. Email is so pressing that many of us find ourselves logging on several times a day. Just deleting the hundred or so spam emails I receive each day carves a huge chunk of time out of my day. So I work longer hours to compensate.

Stop and think about how many people you know where both husband and wife are together, at home, by six or seven at night. How many people leave work at five o clock? How many wives stay at home to mind house and family because the family budget does not need them to earn any money?

These days, most of us choose to work, or work because we have to. Many work away from home. My own husband recently worked overseas during the week for seven years. Most of our friends are in the same boat, or if not, their husbands get home later than the children's bedtimes.

I do not mean to get on my soap-box about this issue but you need motivation if you are to keep getting up in the morning for 48 weeks a year. One of the best ways in the world to do this is to do something you love for a living.

Trying to list all the things you are passionate about can be daunting. Trying to list the things you love might be a little easier, but I bet that listing the things you do *not* like is easiest of all!

We are all unique. Each of us can make a unique contribution to the world and, more specifically, to the workplace. So, think about what special skills, attributes and talents you can bring to a workplace – think of this as your unique contribution. And then, more importantly, I'd like you to think about what you would like in exchange for your unique contribution. Here are some ideas based on myself:

My unique contribution is:

- A talent for writing
- The ability to inspire others
- Creative thinking
- At ease in a multi-cultural environment
- Happy in front of an audience
- Able to absorb and disseminate information

In exchange I require:

- Flexible working hours so I don't miss out on my children
- Opportunity to travel
- Opportunity to work from home
- An office with a view of nature
- To be with people on at least one day a week

TASK FOUR

List here the elements that make up your unique contribution

1

2

3

4

5

List here the elements that you would like to have in exchange for your unique contribution

1

2

3

4

5

List here the things that you do not want to have in your working life, such as late working hours, a commute of more than 30 minutes, an open plan office, working from home and so on.

1

2

3

4

5

TIP FIVE – WHAT DRIVES YOUR CAREER?

In the previous tip we talked about the things you would want to have in your work. Here we are going to dig deeper and talk about what motivates you to work at all in the first place. We need you to be honest with yourself here!

We all have different motives for working. Some people may want money and lots of it, big fat bonus cheques, share options, and regular pay rises. Others may simply want to make a difference to other people or to be able to support and nurture those in need. To some money may be immaterial. Plenty of people want to work just to get out of the house so they do not have to be the sole carer for their children. Some want a label, to be able to say they are a managing director or a chef, for example. Others want to work for a company that is a household name. Some want fame. It maybe that you just want to be a big fish in a small pond, say, to be a mover and shaker in your local community. Or you may want to be famous in your country, or continent, or even throughout the world.

In her book *Transform Yourself*, Ros Taylor explains that there are nine career drivers. These are the catalysts that will get you up in the morning, glad to chip the ice off your windscreen in the dark and answer the phone when you are on holiday. They are:

- Money
- Community
- Power and Status
- Fame
- Spirituality
- Autonomy
- Expertise
- Financial security
- Creativity

Over the years, I have run my Career in Your Suitcase workshops all over the world and am always delighted to hear some more examples of what drives your careers:

- Peace
- Flexibility
- Enough time off
- Work/life balance
- Recognition of achievements
- To feel valued and appreciated
- Networking opportunity
- The chance to be coached or mentored or to be a coach or mentor
- To learn
- Time to watch my children grow

It is important that you enjoy at least some of these drivers in your work, or, if not at work, then in your social or leisure activities. If your work is 'just a job', do you give yourself opportunities to feel fulfilled elsewhere in your life?

TASK FIVE

List here your own career drivers, pick from the list on the previous page or add your own.

1

2

3

4

5

6

Consider whether your current occupation is associated with your career drivers. If so, write down those that you enjoy now.

1

2

3

4

5

6

Look back at your list of career drivers, above, and pick out all those that you do not enjoy in your work, but you do enjoy in your social life or at leisure. Maybe you do not get recognition at work but as president of the local arts society instead? List the career drivers present in your extra curricular activities beside the 'a' column, and name the activity alongside, in the 'b' column.

1a	1b
2a	2b
3a	3b
4a	4b
5a	5b
6a	6b
7a	7b
8a	8b
9a	9b
10a	10b

TIP SIX - FEEL THE FORCE

BE ENERGISED

In her book, *Thriving in Mind*, Dr Katherine Benziger (www.benziger.org) explains that when we are involved in doing something we instinctively love we use only one percent of the energy we normally burn. So, that means, that you may be really good at mathematics at school and get top grades, but that if you were not born to do maths, you would still use up the normal amount of energy doing it. If however, you also love to cook, and cook really well, but find that it comes naturally the chances are that this is your true talent, your true passion, and that you feel energised by the experience.

When you do something and feel great and full of energy afterwards then this may be a clue to the fact that you have found one of your true passions.

I love writing. Most of my work these days is in helping other writers to get their books published and so I do a lot of editing. After four hours editing I am bushed. I need a break, I need fresh air. I love doing it, I'm good at doing it, but it is tiring, focused work.

When I began work on this book. I wrote up to the end of the second tip and had to go and fetch the children from school and had to stop. I was so energised by writing my own book that I sailed through the rest of the evening on a high. I could not wait for this morning when I could start writing again. So you see I love writing but I am passionate about writing my own books.

ENERGY SOURCES

And while I am on the subject of energy, watch out for people who energise you too. If you find that certain people make you feel good when you are around them, then maybe it is because you share similar interests and talk about similar things? Try to surround yourself with people who have found their passions and live by them and some of it will rub off.

TIME FLIES WHEN YOU ARE HAVING FUN

Another clue to help you find your passions is to look out for occasions when time seems to fly. When I'm teaching the day zooms past and I forget to give my students a break for coffee unless they poke me with their pencils and tap their watches menacingly.

When does time fly for you? It could be when you are involved in some aspect of your work, talking to customers, doing the accounts (not me!) or receiving phone calls. Or it could be when you are at home, doing the garden, entertaining friends or tidying cupboards. Whenever you lose all track of time you could be doing something associated with your passion.

Of course, you may enjoy tidying cupboards, but do not feel you could make a career out of it. Well, maybe not, but this might indicate that you like to be organised, that you like to weed out unnecessary items and to be detailed and ordered. Consider any times of domestic bliss and see how you might be able to translate those skills to the workplace.

TASK SIX

List the things that come really easily to you. Not just the things that have given you examination success, but also the things you do in your social life, sport, leisure or play.

1

2

3

4

5

6

List the people you know who make you feel alive and energised when you are around them. Note the things you do or talk about together.

When I am with

_____

we talk about

_____

and we enjoy doing

_____

When I am with

_____

we talk about

_____

and we enjoy doing

_____

When I am with

_____

we talk about

_____

and we enjoy doing

_____

List the things you do at work or play that make time fly

1

2

3

4

5

6

TIP SEVEN - WHAT'S STOPPING YOU?

As I told you in my introduction, I stopped acting when I was 15 because my friends made fun of my achievements. Simple peer pressure. But the other reason I gave up acting was because, at 15, I thought my time was better spent chasing the opposite sex and hanging around in the High Street. Simple hormones, I suppose.

Later, when I was in my early twenties, I did do some more acting. I loved it, the camaraderie of the other actors, the time in the bar afterwards, performing again. I did not feel I was as accomplished nor as confident as I had been as a teenager and when I failed to get a part in the next play my bubble burst. I have not acted since. While the children were young, and my husband worked away from home, my excuse was that I did not want to pay for a babysitter in order to indulge myself in such a frivolity. I told myself that life was too busy for me to find time to learn lines. Then, a couple of years ago, I joined the local amateur dramatic group and paid the annual fee, but never actually attended a meeting. Was I frightened of failure, perhaps, remembering the time when I failed to get a part? Or fear of success, because if I did get a part I would have to find the time to learn lines?

In 2004, at the WIN conference (www.winconference.com) in Lausanne, I had the opportunity to have a free session with a life coach. I picked the life coach who was passionate about acting on purpose. I knew I had to put acting back in my life. Claudia brainstormed the idea with me and together we decided that I would make a point of going to the theatre once every three months and that I would subscribe to *Time Out* magazine, the London magazine that reviews everything that is on in the capital. I kept this up until we left the UK in 2005 and definitely felt more in touch with what was out there.

Now, even though we are in the Netherlands, I still make a point of going to London plays and went to five during 2006 in addition to three in The Hague.

But then my then 11 year old son, Josh, was given the part of Hook in the school production of *Peter Pan*. He had never acted in his life, and though he had bags of confidence, he had little skill. His teacher threatened to recast him. I leapt into action, living vicariously through my child, I turned him into the best Hook he could ever have been. During the rehearsal following my 'treatment' Josh received a round of applause. At last I had found a way to use my passion that did not scare me half to death.

I have still not set foot on a stage again myself, other than as a speaker, but I am fully aware of my passion for acting. I try hard to find ways of putting acting or theatre into my life and enjoying the energy I feel when I get back in touch with my thespian teenage years. It is not easy to hang onto your passion, and in my own life I have seen countless examples when I have sabotaged my happiness.

So, what's stopping you from enjoying the things you are passionate about?

- Lack of time?
- Fear of failure?
- Lack of money?
- Fear of success?
- Peer pressure?
- Not knowing where to start?
- Fear of making a fool of yourself?
- Lack of opportunity?
- Fear of the attention of others?

TASK SEVEN

Think back to times in your past when you have really enjoyed doing something. You have enjoyed it so much that you found the time, the money and moved mountains to maintain your interest. Think of things you did as a child, as a teen, as a young adult and beyond. The things you did before life got in the way. List them here, and then, for each one, consider the reasons why you stopped doing those things and then say how you are going to put it right. What are you going to do about it now?

I used to love

_____

but

_____

so now I am going to put this right by

_____

I used to love

_____

but

_____

so now I am going to put this right by

_____

I used to love

_____

but

_____

so now I am going to put this right by

_____

I used to love

_____

but

_____

so now I am going to put this right by

_____

TIP EIGHT - SUCCESS STORIES

Can you remember some of the successes you have had in your life? The things you achieved or did really well? When did you feel good about yourself? And how did you recognise that you were a success? Did people clap? Did you get letters of appreciation? Did you get a pat on the back, or a bunch of flowers, perhaps? Or simply, did someone say 'thank you'?

Sometimes our success stories can hold more clues to our buried passions. My earliest achievement, I recall, was when, aged six, my poem was read out to my classmates. I think everyone clapped, but if they did not, the fact that I was asked to share something I had done with 30 other pupils was my reward and proved I had succeeded at something. Later, when I must have been about 12, I had written a play about a lost dog and it was performed by my class and shown to the year group.

At university, my writing was published in the college 'rag', so again, my success was measured according to the number of people it affected, but also because my work was selected out of many. Believe me, it was not easy to be published in that paper, there was a lot of competition.

And then I received the copy of the book, *Culture Smart USA*, by Gina Teague. A year earlier I had suggested Gina took the job when the publisher, Kuperard (www.kuperard.co.uk), called me up. I made Gina, a Brit in Australia, who had lived in the USA for many years *believe* she could do it! To date I have helped at least 50 would-be authors get into print.

When I look back at the things I consider to be my achievements it is clear to me that they all involved the following:

- Words – whether I was writing them or speaking them
- Communicating with others in some way
- My work was chosen to be of merit by someone else
- Other people had to 'buy into' my work
- Creativity
- A number of people could read, or watch my work as a result
- Empowering others to believe they are worth something

It is said that if you are to achieve your goals you have to be motivated in some way to go the extra mile. So, for example, if you want to lose weight, you will not do so unless the goal is something you *really* want. Maybe you want to look great at a wedding, at an interview, or squeeze into your favourite jeans?

In order to achieve something you consider to be a success you need motivation. My motivation is and always has been the desire to share what I know, or what I have done with others in order to make them happier, inspired or more fulfilled.

Think of your success stories now. What motivated you to achieve so much?

What allowed you to succeed?

TASK EIGHT

Write a list of your achievements here, not necessarily associated with work. Beside each note down what motivated you to succeed.

I achieved

_____

because

_____

I achieved

_____

because

_____

I achieved

_____

because

_____

I achieved

_____

because

_____

I achieved

_____

because

_____

I achieved

_____

because

_____

I achieved

_____

because

_____

TIP NINE - PORTFOLIO OF PASSIONS

How are you feeling about your quest for the holy grail of long-buried passions? Does it feel achievable now? Are you on the way? I bet if I were to just ask you what you 'loved' rather than what you were 'passionate about' you would find it much easier. I'd get a list – probably beginning with 'chocolate' and including 'time to watch the sunset' and 'laughing with good friends'. Well, the good news is that I don't expect you to identify just one single passion. It's fine to have lots of them.

High performance coach and professional speaker, Steve Head (www.headstart-uk.com), writes about having several passions in his book, *How to Avoid a Near Life Experience*. Steve explains how, after much soul searching he came up with his own four top loves. They were golf, people, communicating and music. Now, he makes playing golf a priority in his spare time and his work allows him to communicate with people all the time. But Steve had a problem when it came to music. He does not play an instrument, so he could not pick up a guitar in the evening and strum away whenever he felt like it. In order to put music into his life he had to be more inventive. His solution was to book a babysitter, permanently, one evening a month so that he and his wife, Abby, could go to a concert or a pub with live music.

It is fine to have a portfolio career, especially if you are freelance. A portfolio career is one where you do several different things that may have little in common, but that allow you to exercise as many of your talents and passions as you can. I have had a portfolio career for more than 20 years now.

Think of all the things you love to do and see if you can find a way to blend as many of them as possible into your life and work.

While you have been exploring have you found that some of the themes that keep cropping up are to do with your family, or your free time? Perhaps you are passionate about being there for your children every evening, about having the time to walk the dog or listening to plays. Each of your passions is just as valuable as another. If you recognise that time off or time in nature is important to you, then ensure you can make time for it somehow. If you do not have time to listen to the radio, why not buy audio-tapes of plays and listen to them in the car or on the train? If you do not have time to walk by the river during the evening, maybe you could take a walk during your lunch hour at work?

You may have to think creatively in order to achieve this, but it can be done. When Jacinta Noonan (www.bigontheinside.com) and I wrote the words and basic tune for a song we call *The Blue Sky Song* my first thought was that I wanted to involve my family. So, I asked my children, Sam and Josh, to give me feedback on the lyrics: 'You can't repeat words like that, Mum. It's not cool,' said Josh. And then my husband, Ian, came up with the definitive chords. Finally, when we all recorded the song, we got my son, Sam on bass, Josh on drums and Ian on lead guitar. That's my way of putting all my passions into play!

TASK NINE

Write down all the things that you would love to do. Do not limit yourself to the things that you know to be possible. Dream a little too. It has been proven that when goals are written down they stand a much better chance of being achieved. Do not stop writing until you have run out of dreams.

_____

_____

_____

_____

_____

_____

_____

_____

_____

_____

Now from the list above, pick four things that you are not doing already, but that you really would be able to do right away without too much of a problem. Remember you can do lots of things concurrently.

1

2

3

4

TIP TEN - DO YOU WANT TO BE ALONE?

Do you think you are an extrovert, or an introvert, or a bit of both? I know that I want to be able to work, alone, in a silent environment. In fact I cannot concentrate on my writing at all if the radio or music is on in the background. This is a sign of an introvert.

My friend Bianca can work and even sleep with music on or people chatting around her. If she is bored for a moment, despite any noise, she falls asleep. I will never forget sitting next to her on an aeroplane. Our friend, Nicki, sat on the other side of her, so we had a row of three seats to ourselves. I was talking to Nicki about work issues and Bianca fell asleep between us. That is a sign of a true extrovert.

Yet I remember that when I lived alone and worked from home for a few months in my twenties, I could not cope with being alone at work and then again in the evening. So, every lunchtime I would go for a walk in the town for an hour, and I always made sure I could be with people in the evenings. 24 hours alone was more than I could handle. I'm not much different now.

Consider your work environment. Do you need to be alone and quiet, like I do? Or would you enjoy the buzz of an open plan office, the chance to chat with your colleagues at the water cooler or coffee machine and to hear the constant ring of telephones?

These days I have my work environment down to a fine art. I spend two days a week working in an office with a small team of people and the rest of the week I work from home or clients' offices. Yet loving travel as I do, I try go overseas for work at least once every other month and run courses away from my home base. In 2006 I worked in Dubai, the Netherlands, Scotland, England and the USA. I attend conferences and networking events too, attend a regular networking group called Connecting Women (www.connectingwomen.nl) once a month and Professional Speakers' Association (www.professionalspeakers.org) meetings. Before I found the part-time work that I now enjoy two days a week I would try to find other people who worked from home and who inspired me and meet them regularly for mutual brainstorms. Best of all, is when I can find someone who inspires me to be a power-walking buddy. Then I can enjoy being outside in nature, getting fit and talking all at the same time.

This book is about finding your passion, but it is important that you also think about how you want to work and live. Could you cope if your office was in a cupboard, like my friend Tracey, who works in her bedroom's walk-in wardrobe? Or do you need a view, like I do. In Oman I could just glimpse the Indian Ocean, in Norway there was a mountain and a hazelnut tree. In England I enjoyed a silver birch and a field full of rabbits.

Would you, like my friend Nicki, who is a freelance journalist and perfectly able to work from home, choose to share an office with other creatives, so that you would have other like-minded people around?

And I'm not just talking about your work environment. Are you a morning person, perhaps, who likes nothing better than to wake up with the sun streaming through your bedroom curtains? Do you like to sit at a window, overlooking a busy street, so that you can watch the world go by? Or does the view not matter to you one jot as long as you can have room for all your possessions or enough bedrooms to have house-parties?

TASK TEN

I want you to read what I write here, and then close your eyes for a full five minutes and picture your perfect work environment. I want you to really be there in the office, or the kitchen, restaurant or wherever for a day. Who is with you? What can you hear? What are people talking about? What kind of desk do you have? What will you eat for lunch? How will your chair feel, the carpet or floor? What will you see out of the window? Imagine it all, use every one of your senses. How will you get to work? What will you wear? What time will you arrive and when will you leave? What will your colleagues be like? Will you be in charge or part of a team?

Now, close your eyes and dream. Go on. Now. Take more than five minutes if you need to.

Now make a note of what you found. Were there things you liked and things you didn't? Write them down here.

TIP ELEVEN – IF MONEY WERE NO OBJECT

Imagine what you could do if you were not tied to a mortgage, young children, elderly parents, the dog, a house to renovate, the need to pay bills or pay off a loan. What could you do if you did not need any money ever again? Perhaps you won the Lottery or inherited a fortune or had a substantial private income. Let's not go mad here, your money needs to last you for at least 30 years, so don't blow it all in one go!

If you could do anything at all. If everything were perfect. If you could have your time again what would you do? Would you do a different degree, perhaps, or would you not bother with education at all?

Imagine that you have no money worries and all the skills you need to do whatever you want. Like magic.

This is genie in the bottle time.

Think about what you wanted to be when you grew up. Would you do that now? Drive a fire engine? Be a pop star?

Think about what you wanted to be when you were aged nine. They say we know what we want to be by then, would you believe?

Think about what you wanted to be when you were a teenager – but before peer pressure or hormones or homework knocked you off track.

Think about what you wanted to be when the world seemed like it was a big place filled with opportunities.

Think about what you wanted to be before that mortgage, children and other things that bound you.

Would you:

- Do one specific job
- Move to a different house
- Do several jobs
- Move to a different area
- Not work at all
- Move to a different country
- Set up a charity or foundation
- Have more children
- Indulge yourself
- Have no children
- Shop
- Travel the world like a nomad
- Fly, sail, run or swim and feel the adrenalin
- Live on a boat, an island, by the sea

TASK ELEVEN

Now you can go mad. Write down here what you would do, or would have done if you did not need money and had all the skills you needed. Remember, anything is possible.

TIP TWELVE - CHILDHOOD INFLUENCES

I wonder whether you had a struggle trying to come up with your values earlier in this book? Sometimes the things we believe in are ingrained in us since birth. We inherit many of our beliefs from our parents and the people who were around us when we were being raised.

For example, you may have been raised in a family where the father, like mine, was a teacher. I thought it was normal for families to take long summer holidays. I remember we used to go to France with the caravan for a month at a time. Then I went to university and still had long holidays. When I started work I was in for a shock. I could not cope with only having four weeks off in an entire year. My body clock expected big fat chunks of time off every few months. To this day I still see my life in 'terms' or 'trimesters'. What happened was that I began to resent every full-time job I had after just a few months. I would feel trapped. So, I would leave. By the time I was 25 I had given up full-time permanent employment forever and gone freelance. This suits me much better.

But am I right? Many would think I am spoiled to expect time off. But few of my close friends would claim that I am lazy. I work 40 hours most weeks, during the school holidays and at weekends sometimes too. I do what I love, but I like to feel I have a choice about when I do it.

'Family inheritance' can stick to you like glue. Sometimes you will consider, as I did, that certain things are normal. In this way, you may think it is normal for a mother to work full-time, part-time or not at all. This may cause you ambivalence when you find yourself in a role that does not match what you are used to.

Think too about what the people who brought you up believed or did. Did they teach you somehow that men work long hours and overseas, like my husband's father? So my husband does the same. Did they teach you that men read the paper every night and women cook the supper, or that work is tough and that you don't enjoy it?

Many such beliefs become ingrained in us too.

But other influences affect us when we are growing up. Not just our parents, but our grandparents too. My grandfather worked until he was 82, and died the next year. My father, at 79 is still going strong, tapping away at his computer and filled with enthusiasm for his work. He even works for me as a Sous Chef.

Teachers can have a great influence. Did you ever find yourself studying a particular subject simply because you liked the teacher? Did you, like me, hate maths, because you disliked that teacher too? I still consider myself number-blind, but I expect it's not true. My games teacher told me I was 'hopeless at all sports, but at least I give everyone a good laugh'. To this day I cannot be persuaded to play any team sport.

And I expect you had a mentor too. Perhaps a family friend, a relative or neighbour. Someone you admired and spent time with. I adored my godmother, Jenny, and realise that it was her passion for cooking for guests that has made me love to do the same.

Who influenced you?

TASK TWELVE

Think for a moment about the people who may have influenced you while you were a child and who may have passed on their beliefs and passions to you.

Name the people who brought you up and influenced you; teachers, parents, carers and mentors.

1

2

3

4

What did they believe about life?

1 _____ believed

2 _____ believed

3 _____ believed

4 _____ believed

What did they believe about work?

1 _____ believed

2 _____ believed

3 _____ believed

4 _____ believed

What were they passionate about?

1 _____ was passionate about

2 _____ was passionate about

3 _____ was passionate about

4 _____ was passionate about

TIP THIRTEEN – START WRITING

SPEEDWRITING

I am a firm believer that speedwriting is a valuable way to get inside yourself and unlock your secrets. Speedwriting has nothing to do with shorthand. Instead it refers to the method by which you write really fast about whatever is on your mind. For this to work you must use a lined notebook with a spiral binding, so it is easy for you to move from page to page. Some people call this kind of writing 'stream of consciousness'.

When you write fast like this, your thoughts may be random – but that's fine. Put down each thought as it comes to you and keep on writing until you have no more to say. Let your mind wander. You must not stop writing to think. If your ideas are slow in coming then write down words such as 'words words words' or 'I must write I must write', but do not take your pen off the paper.

Speedwriting feels like magic. You can almost sense that the thoughts go straight from your soul to the page, bypassing your brain. Lose control, don't worry about spelling, grammar or punctuation. Just write.

In her book about speedwriting, called *Writing Down the Bones*, Nathalie Goldberg talks about the process at length. She says that speedwriting allows your subconscious to emerge and is a great way to find out what you really think and want and believe. As a fan of this method I have to agree. Once I was unsure when to run my next series of creative writing classes. I agonised over the day of the week, the time of the day and the pricing I would use in a new country. So I speedwrote around my thoughts for about 20 minutes, and miraculously, the answer came to me. I would run them on a Thursday morning at 9am. Simple when you know how!

You can speedwrite on any topic you like, of course, and the results can be therapeutic. I even know of several people who formed their own speedwriting group and met monthly to write together and share their experiences. Often it can be very painful to read out loud what you've written. So before you leap into starting a group be careful that you will be among firm friends.

KEEP A JOURNAL

One of the biggest influences on my life has been a book called *The Artist's Way* by Julia Cameron. In fact this was the first workbook I ever completed on my personal journey.

This book is for people who want to unlock their inner creativity and discover who they really are. Yet it is not reserved for artists – we all have creativity in our soul. Cameron asks readers to devote 12 weeks to her course, which includes speedwriting a journal for ten minutes every morning. In addition, Cameron provides a chapter on a different subject each week, asks questions and invites you to reflect on that topic for seven days.

If you get into the habit of writing a diary, like this, you will start to find yourself asking questions and coming up with all kinds of possibilities. If you write your entry first thing in the morning you will remember your dreams and may find hidden messages in them.

TASK THIRTEEN
SPEEDWRITE

Get yourself a spiral bound notebook, or A4 looseleaf pad, a pen you enjoy writing with and a stop watch or timer.

You are going to speedwrite for exactly ten minutes on the subject of 'I love'. Start off by writing just the words 'I love' and then set the timer. Now put your pen on the paper and just go. Just write and write and write. Write fast. Don't worry if you make mistakes or go off at a tangent, but do make sure you keep writing. If your mind goes blank just write 'I love' over and over until an idea comes to you and you can finish the sentence. And that sentence leads to another, and another. When you write fast like this, without censorship, it's as if your pen is hotwired to your heart. It's as if it bypasses your brain and your thoughts.

Other ideas you could use to kick off a speedwriting exercise are:

- The job of my dreams
- When I was a child
- I wish
- In a perfect world
- If I had any money
- If only
- Next year
- Work is
- I am

So, as above, you just need to write down the words you select from the list above, set the timer, put your pen on the paper and go.

START A PASSION JOURNAL

Another way to tune into your innermost desires and your true self is to keep a Passion Journal. At the end of every day, aim to write down:

- When I felt energised today

- When time flew today

- When I felt content today

Write here the date by which you will have bought yourself a nice book to use as your Passion Journal

_____

Write here the date you first began to write in it

_____

TIP FOURTEEN - WRITE YOUR LIFE STORY

Most of us enjoy reading an autobiography. We find them insightful and revealing. So there is every reason for us to write our own in order to find out more about ourselves too.

It is common for career counsellors to ask their clients to begin the self-development process by writing their own life story or career review. When we make an effort to see each of our career choices on paper then we can begin to understand what motivated us to make each decision. It is not uncommon for the process to take several hours. Once you have identified your own career drivers in this way you are in a strong position. You are back in the driving seat.

I would always suggest that you write any of this soul-searching stuff longhand, but, as memories are wont to return randomly you would be forgiven for using a word processor this time.

In her book *Work with Passion*, author Nancy Anderson suggests that you should start writing your own life story by writing about your grandparents, even if you actually never knew them, or hardly saw them. She believes that the thoughts, hopes, dreams and rules of your grandparents are passed down to your parents and from them to you.

She suggests that you write about your grandparents in the third person and use their names, as if to distance yourself from them. My paternal grandparents were Eva and Sydney. They met when my grandmother was 13 and married when my grandfather returned from the First World War. They were very happy. If I think about Eva, I realise that she believed women gave up work as soon as they had a child to devote themselves to the home and family.

Yet when I look at my maternal grandparents, Isobel and Ewen, even though I never knew Isobel I realise how important her work was to her. She taught ballet from home and employed a housekeeper.

My own mother, Jenny, stopped working when my brother and I were small, but once we were old enough to have a house key, she went back to work part-time, first in the evenings and some afternoons and later as a college secretary so she would have the holidays with us. From Jenny I learned that it is important to be there for your children.

Your influences, passions, beliefs, dreams and the rules by which you live your life can come from your grandparents. Even if you never knew them personally, somehow you will have a picture of them and know, deep down, what you think.

If you were not brought up by your blood relations, then you can still complete this exercise, writing about your carers and their families as they will have been just as influential in your life.

TASK FOURTEEN

Now you are going to write your autobiography. You are going to need a separate notebook to complete this task, or to write it at the computer. Leave this page open and refer to it as you write.

Start at the beginning and write about the following in order:

Write about yourself as a child

- What you loved to do
- What frightened you
- Your friends and friendships
- Your family
- Your achievements
- The things you did at play

Write about yourself as a teenager

- What you loved to do
- What frightened you
- Your friends and friendships
- Your family
- Your achievements
- The things you did socially

Write about yourself as a grown up

- Your work
- Your education
- Your leisure time
- Your relationships and why they ended, or why they worked
- What made you happy
- Your successes
- Your failures

- Your passions
- The things you spent most time with and the things you least liked to do

Once you have completed this exercise, and you may have to tackle in it stages, see if you can spot any of the catalysts that caused certain things to happen in your life, the reasons you had arguments with your friends, the reasons you did well in certain subjects and what made you choose them.

When you've finished, look back and see if any patterns emerge. See if this reflection holds some of the keys to what you loved to do.

TIP FIFTEEN - FIND YOUR DEFINING MOMENTS

Dr Phil McGraw is the psychologist doctor who is a regular on the Oprah Winfrey show and has his own show. He has written several useful books to help you understand yourself and your family better. His two books *Life Strategies* and *Self Matters* can be very helpful in a general way.

Dr Phil asks us to identify our Defining Moments, the moments in our lives that shaped us forever. The moments that we can remember clearly with all of our senses.

I can remember distinctly how it felt the day my teacher told me I was too clever for her class. I was six years old and it was my first day in a new school. My new teacher asked me to recite the alphabet. So I did. Perfectly. I did as I had been taught to pronounce the letters *ay, bee, see*. But my teacher said I was wrong and asked me to begin again. I did the same. Then she told me I should have been pronouncing the letters phonetically: *ah, buh, kuh*.

I can still see the disdain on her face, feel the warm September day outside the classroom, remember how cold I suddenly became and how very saddened. This was a defining moment for me and shaped my life. From that moment I thought it was not cool to be clever. At that moment I became 'average'. That was until I was in my twenties, recognised what had happened and allowed myself to achieve once more.

Yet on a happier note, I recall the evening launch party for our *Dates* cookery book in Oman. The room smelled of incense and spice, the guests wore a mixture of eau de nil traditional Omani dress and Western clothes. We ate miniature date and nut cutlets and dates stuffed with ricotta cheese and pine nuts and drank cardamom flavoured Arabic coffee. Outside the window of the Pearl restaurant at the Al Bustan Palace hotel, we could see the sea away through the palm trees. This time I knew I loved the exoticism and opportunity of life abroad and I also knew I could succeed.

Look out for your Defining Moments in your life and career. Sometimes they will be times that made you feel terrific, sometimes they made you sad and sometimes they will have filled you with so much energy that you could almost feel your ego disappear. You were at one with the world.

Take a look at your mental photograph album now, seek out the snapshots that stay clear in your mind and work out what they tell you about yourself today.

Think about moments from:

- Holidays
- Time with your friends
- School
- Early work experience
- Relationships
- Time with family

TASK FIFTEEN

Describe a defining moment from your childhood

_____

What may this have taught you?

_____

How has that affected you today?

_____

Describe a defining moment from your teenage years

_____

What may this have taught you?

_____

How has that affected you today?

_____

Describe a defining moment from your life post education

_____

What may this have taught you?

_____

How has that affected you today?

_____

Describe a defining moment from your work experience

_____

What may this have taught you?

_____

How has that affected you today?

_____

TIP SIXTEEN - ASK YOUR FRIENDS

Sometimes the best way to find out what you love to do and where your passions lie is *not* to stare at your own navel and spend days meditating. Sometimes your assets are staring you in the face and yet you just can't see them! Even if you think you can work out what you love without help from others, I advise that you also ask your friends what they think. You may be surprised.

Several years ago, Canadian Donna Messer (www.connectuscanada.com), then in her forties, left her job as a teacher for a new career that embodied her skills and her passions. When she looked in the mirror she saw only education and experience. She had no idea what she wanted to do, nor what she could do aside from teach. So she asked three of her friends what they saw when they looked at her.

'You make things look nice,' said the first friend, referring to the wonderful decorations Donna would make out of next to nothing to dress up the village hall or her home.

'You make things taste good,' said the second, reminded of the great food Donna would concoct from a random selection of ingredients and spices and serve to the entire football team, when they arrived on an impromptu visit.

'You bring people together' said the third friend, as she recalled the way Donna could organise disparate people into a team and marshal their combined resources to create a successful project.

Thus inspired, Donna went on to create a company called Orange Crate, which sold original combinations of herbs and spices, packed into neat wooden boxes. She also created her team of associates from among the farmers in her community, who felt they could not yet contribute to the business, but offered invaluable help with duties such as driving, deliveries and book keeping.

Orange Crate began with a small loan from a local bank and ten years later was sold to a group of three companies that joined forces to buy it.

'They were a food company, a media company and a financial institution, so we must have done something right!' recalls Donna.

Donna no longer runs Orange Crate. She now travels the world speaking to large groups, conferences and corporations, inspiring them in turn, with her stories of resourcefulness and networking. Since 2000 she has also been editor of the magazine *Business Woman Canada*. She shares her secrets at the Connect Us website

Give your friends permission to share what first springs into their minds when they think about what you are good at. Often first thoughts may seem a little weird, but they are also likely to be accurate, and based on intuition.

TASK SIXTEEN

Ask your friends the following questions:

- What do I love?
- When am I happiest?
- What are my best qualities?
- What are my values?
- What do you value me for?

Now give three of your good friends the chance to answer these questions. Make a note of their names and then keep a record of their answers.

Name of friend

_____

I love

_____

I am happy when

_____

My qualities are

_____

I value

_____

I am valued for my

_____

Name of friend

_____

I love

_____

I am happy when

_____

My qualities are

_____

I value

_____

I am valued for my

_____

Name of friend

_____

I love

_____

I am happy when

_____

My qualities are

_____

I value

_____

I am valued for my

_____

TIP SEVENTEEN - MY HERO!

Who do you most admire? Whenever women are asked this question they frequently feel stumped for a moment. This is largely because, throughout history, there have been fewer female heroines than male. In 2004, when a 75,000 page dictionary of biographies was published, they were telling us on the news that only 12 per cent of entries were for women. So, let's have a think: Emily Pankhurst, Margaret Thatcher, Anita Roddick, Barbara Cassani, Martha Lane-Fox, Boudicca, Joan of Arc, Florence Nightingale... are you getting stuck? Mother Theresa, Ellen MacArthur, Oprah Winfrey... Madonna?

It is not always easy to think of our role models. But I want you to think about yours. Search for them among characters in books, perhaps, among your family and friends, in the workplace, in your own town or community. Someone does not have to be famous in order to be a role model.

I sometimes play the following game with my friends. I ask them to pick someone, among our friends, and explain why they admire them. This certainly makes a change from gossiping! And, you know, if you focus on saying nice things to people they feel good and so do you. Giving compliments is as rewarding as receiving them.

So, let's go back to talking about your friends. I remember doing this with Ian, my husband, once. He picked our friend Pete.

'So, why do you admire Pete?' I asked.

'Because he is a great father, has time to play with his children and seems to really enjoy it,' Ian began. 'And he loves his job, knows he is in the right career, never has any doubts at all. He has a happy marriage, hobbies, really relaxes in company and has a good laugh. And he's down to earth too'

They say that we admire in other people the traits we wish we had ourselves, and that we despise in other people the traits that deep down, we also suffer from. Interesting isn't it?

Now think of the celebrity role models and people from history. Why do you think it is that you admire them? Do you admire Bill Gates because he has made a fortune? Or do you admire him because you know, deep down that he is fairly shy, but had the guts to share a fabulous idea with the world? Do you admire JK Rowling because she is a shrewd entrepreneur, a skilled writer, or because of her rags to riches story?

Speaking personally, I know what I admire in other people is their ability to do work based on their passions, to be content wherever they are and with whatever they have, to have a work-life balance, to be witty and intelligent. And I despise laziness and meanness. Remember what I wrote earlier? Not only do I fear I suffer from those traits, but I am passionate and admire their converse: action and generosity.

And who are my heroes? The late John Diamond, because he was the most fantastic journalist in the world; Christy Nolan the disabled poet, because he made it as a writer against all odds; Gustave Flaubert, for writing the most beautifully orchestrated prose based in France; Cliff Richard for being authentic. I think I see a pattern emerging!

TASK SEVENTEEN

Who are your heroes or heroines from history and why?

My Hero/Heroine is

_____

because

_____

My Hero/Heroine is

_____

because

_____

My Hero/Heroine is

_____

because

_____

Who do you admire among your friends and why?

I admire

_____

because

_____

I admire

_____

because

_____

Who do you admire from contemporary news, politics, arts or sport for example and why?

I admire

_____

because

_____

I admire

_____

because

_____

And what do you despise in people?

_____

_____

_____

_____

_____

TIP EIGHTEEN – HOW TO MAKE YOUR PASSION PAY

For many years I have been advocating the benefits of creating a career based on passion. But frequently someone in the audience puts up their hand to ask: 'So how do you suggest that I can find and follow my passions when I am a single mother and work full-time?'

To this I usually suggest much as I did earlier in this book, during the introduction. Many of us need a job to pay the bills, but may still be able to contemplate having a very part-time career too. Over time, as the career builds momentum and income, the job can be reduced, until, one day you only do work you love.

It may seem a bit idealistic, but it is possible if you are willing to put in the effort. If you devoted just one hour a day to your career you would notch up more than 360 hours (that's 45 working days) during a year. The trick to building a business that grows as if by magic is to find a way of generating passive revenue. If you own a few properties and let them out, the rental income is passive revenue.

If you write a book and set up mechanisms to keep it selling, then the book sales create passive revenue. If you become a distributor for a company like Forever Living (www.forever-living.com) or Tupperware (www.tupperware.com) and recruit other distributors for your team, they earn money for you as well as themselves – the bigger your team the more passive revenue you earn.

Of course, you can aim to run some kind of business, or find work that allows you to exercise your passions, but does not create passive revenue. But wouldn't it be fantastic if it did?

Here are some examples of my passive revenue streams:

- I write books to sell at my workshops and speaking engagements
- I turn the books into ebooks and sell them on the Internet
- I turn my course notes into ebooks and ecourses
- I record my talks and put them on CD to sell
- I recruit people to buy my books at discount and sell on for me

INTRODUCING PENNY THE PASSIONATE PIG

As soon as someone told me that the term for this is a Passive Income Generator, I saw the acronym quite clearly as a pig. I believe that the best PIG you can create is one based on your passions, therefore it is a passionate pig. My friend Fiona suggested that she be called Penny.

To remind yourself that your ultimate goal is a Passionate Pig, buy yourself a pink toy or ceramic pig and sit it on your desk. Or draw yourself a picture:

My son, Sam, designed me this Penny:

TASK EIGHTEEN

By now you should have worked out where at least some of your passions lie. I want you to note three of them down here, and then concentrate on each of them for a few minutes, blue sky and brainstorm with yourself until you have come up with some ways that you could create some passive revenue from it. It does not matter how little you know about the subject, nor how wild it may seem, just go mad!

Passion:

Passionate PIGs

_____

_____

_____

_____

Passion:

Passionate PIGs

_____

_____

_____

Passion:

Passionate PIGs

_____

_____

_____

_____

TIP NINETEEN – PASSION ON YOUR MIND

THE WISDOM OF CHILDREN

In November 2003, when I attended the UK Professional Speakers' Association (www.professionalspeakers.org) convention, I was lucky enough to hear Molly Harvey (www.mha-training.com) talk about the power of the storyboard. She explained how by sticking a photo of her own head onto Carol Vorderman's body and fixing it onto the fridge door she dropped a dress size.

On the Sunday afternoon, when I came back from the convention, I told my children about the storyboard and how it could make some dreams come true. Then we made our own. I found a large cork board and planted a pile of old magazines, coloured paper, felt tip pens, scissors and pins on the table. Dividing the board into four, I said we'd each have our own corner and that we could do whatever we wanted, make up any pictures, write any words or cut out any mad shapes we liked, to represent our dreams, however wild or wonderful. We called our board The Dream Board.

Sam is no sportsman, but he put a pair of running shoes on his quarter of the board. 'To make me better at sport,' he said. And he put on a picture of an electric guitar: 'To make me better at the guitar.' He cut out a sofa and drew a stick man, representing himself, on it to make him have 'more time to rest after homework'. And then there was a shiny bed, some strawberries and various other things.

Josh cut out a huge picture of a rugby champion. 'Because I want to be a rugby champion,' he said. He drew a musical note with a smiley face in it 'because I want to start being happy about practising my saxophone'. Then his face went all serious. He started

93

hunting about in all the kitchen drawers. Soon he found a photo of himself with his mates, all pulling silly faces and put that in his section.

'I want to be a better friend, too,' he said.

Before long the board was crammed with photos, words and symbols.

A few weeks later, Josh was practising his sax three times a week. He got into the A team for rugby. Things were hotting up! His bedside lamp had been broken for about six months. Ian had never got round to fixing it. I thought it was a boy's job and ignored it.

'If you don't fix my light this weekend I'm putting it on The Dream Board,' hurrumphed Josh to his dad. Ian fixed his light.

In 2003 Sam came 70th in the school cross country competition, out of 80. After the dream board, in 2004, he came 49th. What a score!

On my quarter of the board I pasted a picture of a red rose, because I wanted time to smell the roses, a sunset beach scene, because I wanted to take more time off to sit and think and look at nature, a microphone, because I wanted to be a better speaker.

Perhaps you could create yourself a Passion Board, filled with illustrations, pictures, words and symbols that will help you to keep your passions in sight at all times?

TASK NINETEEN

Let's pretend that the page below is your Passion Page. Get yourself some coloured pens and attempt to fill the paper with images, symbols and words that represent your passions. Really be creative. Then, when you have practised here, and seen how looking at this page makes you feel, start to plan a real Passion Board and put it up where you can see it every day.

TIP TWENTY - CHECK FOR THE SIGNS

HAVE YOU FOUND YOUR PASSION?

In 2003 I gave the talk I call 'Find Your Passion' to 80 or so expatriate women at the American Women's Club (www.fawco.org) in Amsterdam. It was a fabulous building, a vast church-like room and a super place to give a presentation. And it was a sunny day outside, so that may have had something to do with it, but I really felt the audience was with me that day. But the day had started less well.

I had arrived late with only five minutes to spare but it was not supposed to be that way. I had decided, foolishly, to walk to the venue rather than take a tram. Five minutes after leaving the train station I dropped, and lost my map. I had to guess the way there, based on memory and instinct.

Now, I am one of those women who can read maps and does have a good sense of direction, so my goal was not too ludicrous. But I got lost. Time was running out.

Eventually, after crossing about ten canals, I plucked up the courage to ask someone on a bike for directions. He had a pile of parcels with him so had to be a courier of some kind. He was helpful but I was soon lost again. In desperation I began asking passers by for directions every couple of minutes.

Anyway, with five minutes to my talk, and rather flustered from dragging my case over so many cobbles and hump backed bridges I arrived at the venue for my talk. Instinct and determination to handle it without the aid of map or public transport I had made it.

The lobby was crammed with people who all knew each other, but I found a table with the words Welcome Table marked on it and went over. Within seconds I had a cup of coffee in my hand and felt among friends.

Forty-five minutes later, my talk was over. Time had flown. Despite having no props, no overhead projector and a half page of notes, I had never been lost for words. It all came naturally. They seemed to have liked it. I'd made them laugh, made them think and everyone had seemed attentive.

'Are there any questions?' I asked, scanning the room for a pair of eyes to meet mine and a hand to raise.

'When are you coming back?' someone called out.

Afterwards, in high spirits, I went on to chat to many of the attendees as they put their name on the list to receive my newsletter and the notes. A sizeable number of them also bought copies of my books. I was also paid for doing the talk, which is always a bonus.

Then I realised I was having an Aha moment. Here I was, talking about finding your passion, when, quite clearly, everything told me I had found mine. I felt at home. It felt right, I had relied on my instinct and I had been myself.

TASK TWENTY

Finding your passion can be tough, but once you have found it, you may need, like me to stop for a while and look at what you are doing, and just check that you have got it right.

It may be a while before you can complete this page, but once you feel that you are on track, have maybe found your passionate PIGs and are making money from doing what you love, here are some pointers, that I call Passion Posts, to help you.

JO'S TEN PASSION POSTS

1) Do you feel that you get where you need to be sometimes as if by magic, or instinct? Do you no longer use a map?

2) Are you happy to ask for help, support, advice or directions? And can you spot who to ask?

3) When you do your work, does it feel familiar, and comfortable, without fear or nerves, like coming home?

4) While you do what you do are people listening, paying attention, being inspired?

5) As a result of your work do you think you make a difference; make people think differently?

6) Do you get great feedback and get paid? Do you find people willingly give you testimonials and endorsements, even referrals, sometimes without asking?

7) When you do your work, does it feel natural, as if you were born to do this?

8) Do you find that people you meet want to stay in touch with you? Do they ask you for your card, rather than you give it to them anyway?

9) Do you find that people want to buy your products or services and that you rarely have to do a hard sell?

10) When you do what you do, do you walk on air, does time fly? Are you 'in the zone'?

CASE STUDIES

KATE ATKIN

40-year old Kate Atkin decided to make her dream a reality when her mum developed cancer. These days she makes her living helping others do just that: make their dreams a reality with her own business, Aspire 2.

ME AND MY PASSIONS:

I have four passions. My first is a combination of inner beliefs, thoughts and confidence. These were always a love of mine, but the more I worked on them for myself, the more I came to realise that they're fundamental to everyone. My second is eco-friendliness and sustainability. I think it's really important that we look after our environment. Perhaps this comes from my farming upbringing? I recently joined a local sustainability group and I promote ideas to friends as well as adapting my own behaviour to be more eco-friendly – recycling everything I possibly can down to the last Post-it™ note and using busses, cycling shorter distances rather than taking the car. I was lucky enough to speak about the topic at a Rotary dinner recently and was overwhelmed, not just by the energy the subject invokes in me, but by the number of people who are unaware of the issues. My third passion is dancing simply because I love the feeling it creates and my fourth is to keep learning.

ABOUT MY CAREER:

I run my own training business called Aspire 2, which develops individuals and organisations, or, as I like to say, is all about 'transforming aspirations into reality', which has become the company's tagline. Setting up my own business has given me the freedom and flexibility I always yearned. It means I can choose where and when I work, how much holiday I take and it also gives me the opportunity to send myself on workshops, so that I am developing constantly, which helps me to keep the passion burning.

HOW I FOUND MY PASSION:

The ball started rolling as I sat at work one day. At the time, I was an international manager for Barclays Bank in Cambridge. I realised that I had learned a multitude of skills during my membership of Junior Chamber International (www.jciuk.org.uk) but the majority of them simply were not being put to use in my job. I had also completed a train the trainer workshop and had started competing in debating and public speaking competitions, which I really enjoyed. So I applied for a new job on the training team. I got it and found that somehow, it just fitted.

After three years, I set up on my own, although the timing of this decision was spurred largely by my mum's condition. My mum had developed cancer and I made the decision at a time that would ensure she would see me make a success of the business. The decision was also made with an offer of two days' work. As it turned out, it only ended up being one day and was scheduled a month later than expected. By then I had already made my decision, which I knew was the right one and I haven't looked back since.

To this day, I make a point of constantly learning, which

keeps the fire in my belly burning. I'm a member of the PSA (www.professionalspeakers.org), I regularly take part in Toastmaster (www.toastmasters.org) competitions and keep going to workshops and reading books.

HOW I MADE MY PASSION MY REALITY:

I eventually found my passion by working with what gave me a buzz, what I found inspiring and where my gut told me I should be going. Financially, it was a huge risk but I decided not to wait until I met someone who could support me, but to just go for it. Something inside told me it would work out and I knew I could always get a job in a supermarket or something to tide me over if necessary.

Handing in my notice to Barclays was the really scary bit – I did it at a team away day and realized right away that it was the people I would miss rather than the job itself. Once I'd made my decision, although some nerves remained, there was also a sense of excitement. I looked forward to the unknown and knew on a practical level that I could find a job if I really had to – even if it was just filling shelves!

I always knew my business would work out and the gut feeling of 'it's the right move to make' stayed with me. I felt very nervous cold-calling an HR manager following an introduction from some of her staff who had been at a conference at which I was speaking. But I picked up the phone all the same. During the call she told me that I had been their favourite speaker. I was absolutely delighted and this gave me the encouragement I needed to stay on track. On the spot I offered to go in and talk to her about their training needs. This was to be the start of a relationship that continues today and I am very proud of what we have achieved together.

WHO HELPED ME ON MY WAY:

My list is endless but the main starting points that got me going were:

- JCI UK (www.jciuk.org.uk).
- Jack Black, *Mindstore for Life*, Balloon View Ltd.
- Susan Jeffers, *Feel the Fear and Do it Anyway*, Ballantine Books / Vermilion.
- My close friends, Angie and Catherine were a huge help as were my mum and my dad.
- My sister Sharon, who died at the age of 24, was also an inspiration and,
- *Dead Poets Society*, starring Robin Williams.

THE DIFFERENCE A BIT OF PASSION HAS MADE TO MY LIFE:

Before finding my passion I was a quiet person, although deep down, I always knew there was something inside me wanting to get out – I just didn't know how to let it out and wasn't even sure it would be safe. Before starting up on my own, the only thing I lacked was courage; I had no shortage of ideas or information I needed. In the end I just acted on instinct. My.internal voice grew so loud I could not ignore it any more.

These days, I enjoy my life. I find myself very busy, often working long hours and away from home but I have the freedom to take a day off exactly when I want to. And most of the time, I love what I do. There are still times when the nerves creep back and loneliness occurs, but that's not often.

Contact me on: kate@kateatkin.com

Take a look at my website: www.aspire-2.com

NADIYA DAY

Nadiya Day lived in Milan, Italy, for eleven years before returning to the UK in September 2005. Spurred on by her partner contracting AIDs, Nadiya turned her life around and began helping other people address their emotional disabilities. She started her own company, Balanced Living, which uses the latest in mind-body sciences to help people transform subconscious resistance to change, enabling them to achieve their full potential.

ME AND MY PASSIONS:

I'm passionate about beauty, justice and discovering who we truly are. I believe we are here to be happy. My passions all relate to the areas of health, wellbeing and performance. My aim is to inspire us all to invest in 'real health' and develop our natural abilities, preferably through effective, empowering techniques, that can be easily fitted into a busy schedule.

ABOUT MY CAREER:

Prior to becoming self-employed I worked in fashion, marketing, interior design, housing and the health sector. I then spent several years as a feng shui and space-clearing consultant.

My work now involves raising awareness about the benefits of investing in wellbeing. So many people are not living life to its potential and are held back by limiting beliefs and emotional baggage. Our lives are a reflection of our beliefs and our beliefs are 95% sub-conscious and so I work with clients helping to identify those unhelpful beliefs and replace them with supportive ones aligned with their goals and dreams.

105

I started Balanced Living several years ago to achieve this and work with individuals and organisations that want to be happier, healthier and improve performance. We provide training, workshops, coaching and one-to-one and group sessions in stress management, wellbeing and emotional health. We use the latest in body-mind science and quantum mechanics to address stress, raise energy levels and exchange outdated patterns of behaviour for more helpful models.

For example, one of the most empowering energy psychologies I use is Emotional Freedom Technique (EFT), an easily learned, self-applied acupressure technique, which helps release negative emotions, memory and trauma as well as physical and emotional pain and stress. When addressing stress I also consider environmental stressors, using kinesiology (muscle/energy testing) to demonstrate the weakening or strengthening effect of objects and environments on the inhabitant.

The discovery of another psychological process, called PSYCH-K™, which complements EFT, has been life-changing for both my clients and myself. Its originator Robert M Williams MA, says that PSYCH-K™ is "a user-friendly way to rewrite the software of your mind in order to change the printout of your life". PSYCH-K™ uses kinesiology to communicate directly with the subconscious mind to identify these beliefs. Typically, I work with these techniques and follow them with a simple set of whole-brain processes to complete the process.

HOW I FOUND MY PASSION:
I think my start in life has had a lot to do with who I have become and how my passion has evolved. My birth father was Jamaican and my mother French/Russian. My mother left me when I was five days old and I spent six months in

care before being adopted by a loving family. I believe I chose this experience in this lifetime to help me find my life path and see this as a gift. They say you teach what you most need to learn. I have always been motivated to discover who I really am, to release birth trauma and unhelpful patterns of behaviour learned or passed on from both sets of parents.

Then, in the 1980's my partner was diagnosed with AIDS and we began researching the best ways to boost the immune system and transform negative emotional and physical pain. We also looked at the life lessons and opportunity this situation created in our lives. I started working for a pioneering organisation in the area of HIV and housing and became fascinated by the concept of a living/wellness home.

I think my passion found me. I knew there must be a better way of treating and preventing the physical and emotional suffering I saw around me. The turning point came when I had two incredible readings by a well-known psychic and an astrologer. I was astonished by the detail and accuracy of both my character and past experiences. Both readings said that I would be working in the field of wellbeing and personal performance, and that I should train seriously in this area, and mentioned the impact this would have on my life and on others.

Initially, I did one of the first UK courses in feng shui to train as a practitioner. My aim was to show clients how their homes and workplaces could reduce stress and increase energy levels and create a sense of wellbeing. I noticed that some feng shui consultants and books were provoking fear rather than inspiring people to make healthy choices. However, I felt feng shui failed to address the underlying beliefs, which were frequently causing or contributing to problems and that something else was needed to help people to change at a deeper level. It was then that my focus switched from the environmental to the human energy field.

HOW I MADE MY PASSION MY REALITY:

I moved to Milan in 1994 and worked for a breast cancer organisation out there, which led me to develop the Breast Health & Vitality workshop, to raise awareness of the connection between our life-style choices and health. I continued training in various healing modalities, learning about the human energy field and researching effective change-processes and energy boosting techniques. Discovering energy psychologies and whole-brain techniques was a turning point in my practice as a wellbeing and vitality coach. Long-term vision, determination, faith and being true to myself have been the most important factors in making my passion my reality.

WHO HELPED ME ON THE WAY:

Living in Italy for 11 years helped me develop as a woman, a teacher and a speaker. In 2005 I was 'guided' to move back to the UK, which was something that I thought I would never do – I've learnt never to say 'never'. The following have all helped me get to where I am today:

The WIN Global Leadership Forum, (www.winconference.net). This wonderful conference provided an opportunity to make some amazing contacts and friends and do some rewarding work. I was able to pilot my Energy Workout Sessions™ at WIN's early morning Awakening Sessions and as a result these workouts are now held at international events and conferences.

The Wellbeing Network, (www.wellbeingnetwork.co.uk). This amazing initiative is going to revolutionise wellbeing in the next few years.

Bruce Lipton Phd, *The Biology of Belief*, Cygnus Books.

Robert M Williams MA, *PSYCH-K™, The Missing Piece in Your Life*, Myrddin Publications.

Donna Eden, *Energy Medicine*, Piatkus.

David Feinstein, Donna Eden and Gary Craig, *The Healing Power of EFT & Energy Psychology*, Piatkus Books.

Esther and Jerry Hicks, *Ask and it is Given - the Teachings of Abraham*, Hay House.

David R Hawkins, MD, PhD *Power Versus Force*, Veritas Books.

Patricia Carrington PhD, *The Book of Meditation*, Element Books.

Masuru Emoto, *The Hidden Messages in Water*, Pocket Books.

Eckhart Tolle, *The Power of Now*, Hodder and Stoughton.

John Diamond MD, *Life Energy & The Emotions: How to Release your Hidden Power*, Eden Grove Editions.

Daniel J Benor MD, *Spiritual Healing: Scientific Validation of a Healing Revolution*, Vision Publications.

Samuel Epstein MD and Dr David Steinman, *The Breast Cancer Prevention Program*, Macmillan.

Dr Peter J D'Adamo, Catherine Whitney, *Eat Right for Your Type*, Century Books.

THE DIFFERENCE A BIT OF PASSION HAS MADE TO MY LIFE:

Living my passion has enriched my life enormously. It's been a fascinating journey of discovery, which led me to ways of healing the effects in my life of being 'abandoned' at birth. I am now able to change any beliefs which hold me back and replace them with those I desire in any area of my life. I consider myself a work in progress. I continue to feel healthier, have more energy, focus, inner peace and confidence.

Whilst I am fortunate that I am constantly reminded of how beautiful people are, I am also saddened that so much of our potential remains undiscovered and untapped – that many of the people I work with have been literally 'dis-abled' by limiting beliefs and unnecessary emotional baggage. Often the true extent of their 'emotional disabilities' is kept hidden from friends, family and colleagues, which creates additional stress. As time passes it becomes easier to perceive this disempowered state as normal and permanent. My passion and fire helps me to shine light on the situation and I offer solutions that work. I am able to help my friends and family and make a difference to my clients' lives and that's a real honour and extremely satisfying.

Contact me on: NadiyaDay@Balanced-Living.eu

Tel: +44 (0)20 8141 4697 or +44 (0)7726 927 327

Take a look at my website:
www.InfiniteEnergyHealth.com

JEANNE HEINZER

42-year old Jeanne Heinzer is German and lives in The Hague, in the Netherlands, with her Swiss husband and two children. Understanding what really drives her helped her carve out a career as an intercultural trainer, where she now puts her love of languages and people contact to use on a daily basis.

ME AND MY PASSIONS:

My passions are foreign languages and people, particularly anyone who finds themselves living in a country, which is not their own, as I do.

ABOUT MY CAREER:

I now have my own business, Heinzer Consulting, which enables international managers and their partners to live happier lives while living abroad. I am an intercultural coach and trainer, accompanying mobile people through their transition and assignment to allow them to make the most of it, personally and professionally. I work on a freelance and self-employed basis, which is great as it gives me the flexibility to decide whether or not I want to take on a project.

My work means I also get to travel; another of my passions. Although my intercultural workshops don't pay terribly well, they do allow me to break out of my routine and give me the perspective and distance I need to take a look at my own life. I offer a bespoke service, tailored exactly to the intercultural needs of a particular client and work with individuals, couples and accompanying partners. Combining my training with a coaching approach my clients learn about the new country in which

111

they find themselves but often they learn as much about themselves in the process.

HOW I FOUND MY PASSION:

It took me some time to find out that I needed a job where I can work with foreigners on a regular basis. I found my passion a long time ago, when I studied languages (English and French) in Germany. But although I managed to live my primary passion of languages, I had to go through a personal crisis to fully understand that I am primarily a people person.

I had been working as a communications manager for a chemical company in Basel and although some people had warned me that this job would be too technical for me, I didn't listen to them. However, after two years I was really fed up of sitting in front of a PC and not working *with* people. I was close to burn out, working full time and studying communications in London, when I finally realised that I had to take a dramatic decision. It was at that time that a good friend said to me, "Du musst für etwas brennen, damit Du nicht ausbrennst!" which roughly translates as "you have to burn for something so that you don't burn out". Her words came at just the right time. The decision was to leave both public relations, which I felt was much too superficial for me, and the corporate world, opting instead to move back into self-employment.

I realised that it is not enough to train people or to be considered the expert providing them with answers to their questions. I must help them to find their own unique answers by asking questions. So what I do now is to combine training with a coaching approach. Depending on the circumstances in the training room I adapt my own style to meet my participants' requirements. My objective is to allow them to leave the room thinking: this has really added value to me.

HOW I MADE MY PASSION MY REALITY:

The toughest thing was having to cope with the internal struggle and voice nagging away at me saying, "but Jeanne, you have invested so much in your career in communications, you can't just stop it now." But I knew there was a high price to be paid if I stayed in the corporate world, including the loss of my freedom and a sacrifice in terms of my independence and creativity. The crucial change happened when I realised that instead of using the skills I had learnt for others, I could use them for myself.

I already had the personal experience of being an accompanying partner and working in five European countries I had worked with almost every nationality on earth. I felt that the time was right to bring it all together. When I was approached by an intercultural service provider, offering settling in and acculturation advice to those new to an overseas posting, and asked to be her co-trainer for a British guy moving to Germany. I was a complete novice. I had never done this kind of work before, and she just handed me the folders.

I prepared over the weekend, delivered the training and loved it. The training went so well that the same lady approached me again when I had just moved back to Switzerland and asked if I could be their intercultural trainer over there. I agreed instantly and flew to London for training. They did not pay for my trip, nor for the accommodation, so I had to invest a lot of my own money into the project. It was definitely worth it.

Before stopping work in the corporate world, I had saved quite a bit of money and initially I scaled down from a full-time job to working half time, which helped me overcome the financial shock. Slowly, I have managed to work my way up to a position where I am totally independent.

Taking a course in coaching was the real eye-opener and I now consider myself an intercultural coach, trainer and facilitator and have my own business, Heinzer Consulting, which enables international managers and their partners to live happier lives while living abroad.

When I made the change I knew it was right because it just fitted; I didn't need to think about whether it was right or wrong. The feedback I was getting from participants also proved that I was on the right path.

People often ask me about my educational background. My background is not academic but based on experience. Having the courage to live many lives in one life is my personal recipe. I believe that as an intercultural trainer life experience is almost more important than the educational background.

I became a good trainer by training, training and training. Of course, it really helped to have a PR background as I knew how to sell myself and my services. I also feel that it is very valuable to have worked in five or six different industries. As a trainer I constantly work in different company environments and can consequently easily relate to people. It is also helpful that I have experience of life abroad as a single, couple and as a family, because it adds credibility to every single mission. I make sure I continue educating myself in both coaching and NLP.

WHO HELPED ME ALONG THE WAY:

Cendant Intercultural Services (https://homepage.cartus.com/) who trained me to become one of their trainers.

Jo Parfitt, *A Career in Your Suitcase*, Summertime Publishing.

The Professional Women's Group in Basel (http://www.pwg-basel.ch/)

Accompanying partners and companies in Switzerland who trusted me.

THE DIFFERENCE A BIT OF PASSION HAS MADE TO MY LIFE:

Finding and working with my passion now means that my life just feels so right. I am following my own path and that's what's important, putting my own unique gifts to good use. Pursuing my passion has helped me to overcome my own hurdles and deal with my own challenges. Helping others to deal with transition proves to be the best remedy for myself; I learn so much from my participants that it helps and forces me to put my own feelings about living abroad into words and into messages for them.

With my own life as transient as it is my passion has proved my personal anchor. It has forced me to integrate more consciously, as I need to be able to walk my talk.

Contact me on: jheinzer@heinzerconsulting.com

Take a look at my website:

www.heinzerconsulting.com

PAT REEVES

Pat Reeves is a 62-year old British citizen living in the West Midlands. Despite inheriting osteosarcoma (bone cancer), Pat has succeeded in living life to the full. She runs a business in nutritional and functional medicine, holds the British, European and World records in power-lifting and has just created a new unequipped record for the British Drug Free Power-lifting Association (BDFPA). She became the World Champion Power-lifter in November, 2006

ME AND MY PASSIONS:

During my life, I have come to realise that passions change. For a long time, and absolutely at present, my passion is to devote whatever time remains to me to furthering the health of my patients and maintain, as far as possible, a high-quality productive, inspired life that touches others. Writing my book on how it all happened is also high on my list of passions. Honestly, I think passion found me; divine intervention placed me in a position where it was all too obvious I'd been given it assuredly.

Power-lifting is another total passion and has been since I changed from winning marathons in the late eighties. I won my first power-lifting competition in 1989 and have gone on to win around ninety since then. I have retained my sixteen-year BWLA (The Official British Weightlifting Association) record and have just gone on to win the title of World Champion Power-lifter. I refuse to believe I will be forced to stop competing in world events, despite contracting cancer.

ABOUT MY CAREER:

I love what I do and I do what I love and I do my utmost to avoid doing anything that does not qualify. My business is nutritional and functional medicine, which entails a complete assessment of previous dietary input, lifestyle values, present and past symptoms and an assessment of nutritional deficiencies, intolerances and biochemical status. Most days I am busy assisting patients with their health and emotional challenges and this in turn enriches my own life. I train and coach athletes and non-athletes alike and cover all eventualities within these twin aspects. I have adopted a raw-vegan lifestyle with total passion, which I impart to others. I also make use of naturopathic techniques, which embrace rehabilitation, physical medicine, homeopathy and herbal medicine, biotherapeutic drainage and auricular medicine.

HOW I FOUND MY PASSION:

Before finding my passion, I worked as a fashion designer and PA to a photographic expert. The turning point, which caused me to arrive at my life's purpose was inheriting terminal, genetic cancer of the bones. I took all the appropriate steps to be trained in naturopathic and nutritional medicine and studied several other therapies, in order for me to offer an ever-widening knowledge to facilitate my patients' ongoing wellbeing. The fact that it has become a career is purely incidental. I just want to be instrumental in giving love, hope and improved health to all who consult me.

HOW I MADE MY PASSION MY REALITY:

Realising my passion meant a total change of lifestyle and though this was initially tough, it has become much easier, including switching to my completely raw-vegan diet.

WHO HELPED ME ALONG THE WAY:

Books and people, too numerous to mention, have helped me along the way and virtually all of my training was in place before I even knew about the internet. But I would like to mention:

Living Foods (www.livingfoods.co.uk)

The Fresh Network (www.fresh-network.com)

Beata Bishop, *A Time to Heal*, First Stone Publishing – I can only hope my life may be further extended to produce a similarly inspirational book.

Overall, I would say it is my faith and acknowledgment of the Almighty's guidance that has made me who I am. Getting to grips with the real me is essentially an ongoing process and self-improvement never ends.

THE DIFFERENCE A BIT OF PASSION HAS MADE TO MY LIFE:

Finding my passion has meant I have transformed from an average working mother with little ambition to an inspired therapist seeking to prolong my life and that of others. Leading by example, I express my gratitude daily for both the continuance of my life and my ability to help others. My focus is certainly more spiritual than forty years ago. All I can say is that going for it worked for me!

Contact me on pat@foodalive.org

Take a look at my website: www.foodalive.org

DIANA STORE

British-born Diana Store lives in Amsterdam, where she has created a career from her healthy lifestyle. Her own passion for raw foods made her feel so good that she stopped keeping her secret to herself.

ME AND MY PASSIONS:

My passion is everything to do with raw foods and living an optimally healthy lifestyle.

ABOUT MY CAREER:

For many years healthy eating and raw foods were simply a part of my personal lifestyle. I now have a slot on the Noordermarkt for one day a week, which is the organic farmers' market in Amsterdam, selling wheatgrass, books, special foods and equipment that is useful to people eating similarly to me. I organise events including seminars and dinner parties, as well as giving workshops in the art of preparing delicious raw foods. I have invited many of the best-known raw food authors and speakers to Holland, which have been really fantastic experiences for me, and everyone who comes to an event.

Currently I am collaborating with some of these experts on a book, which describes all the commonly agreed upon principles of how to successfully implement a raw food diet. I am also working on my own independent book, *Raw Superfoods* describing cacao (raw chocolate), maca, goji berries and wheatgrass, and how to use them in an everyday diet. I also give private classes or lifestyle coaching to individuals who want more special support. Slowly I have added to my product line and recently launched a webshop at www.rawsuperfoods.com.

What started out as a very personal journey has transformed into an extremely varied and often demanding job.

HOW I FOUND MY PASSION:

I discovered my passion when I was visiting a friend in the Cayman Islands in 1996, and read the book *Fit for Life,* by Harvey and Marilyn Diamond. I dropped all the junk, processed and animal foods from my diet, started consuming a lot of vegetable juices and made 70% of my daily diet fresh, uncooked foods. I immediately gained the benefits of more energy, more positive moods, better sleep and greater immunity to common illnesses. I was so impressed by these results that I developed a burning desire to tell as many people as possible about it.

At the time I was working in the field of landscape architecture and moved to Amsterdam in 2001 to work on the urban renewal plans for Amsterdam North. When I arrived, I could not find any of the services related to the raw-foods lifestyle, which I had experienced elsewhere, so I decided to start something myself. The feeling grew and grew until it became my primary career motivation and I stopped working as a landscape architect and started my business Raw Superfoods.

HOW I MADE MY PASSION MY REALITY:

First of all I had to read a lot to be sure that all my own dietary decisions were the best they could be. Then I had to learn how to make the food interesting and tasty enough, both to satisfy myself and to be able to share it with others. Spending time in the United States in 2002 and 2006 where there is a very established raw food movement and visiting centres such as the Hippocrates Health Institute in Florida and the Tree of Life Rejuvenation Centre in Arizona has given me a lot of ideas.

At about the time I started Raw Superfoods in 2003, I was offered very cheap accommodation in a North Holland village. It was 'anti-kraak' (Dutch for 'anti-squatting') which is when a building owner lets out their empty house at a low price to prevent squatters breaking in. Amazingly, this situation lasted three and a half years, which gave me the opportunity to grow my business without normal living expenses holding me back.

WHO HELPED ME ALONG THE WAY:

Brian Clement, director of Hippocrates Health Institute (www.hippocratesinst.com) and author of *Living Foods for Optimum Health*, Prima Life.

Dr Gabriel Cousens, Rainbow Green Live Food Cuisine and Spiritual Nutrition, North Atlantic Books, and director of Tree of Life Rejuvenation Centre, (www.treeoflife.nu)

David Wolfe, Nutritionist, *Eating for Beauty*, *Nature's First Law and Sunfood Diet Success System*, Maul Brothers.

David and Marilyn Diamond, *Fit for Life*, Bantam.

Nomi Shannon, *Raw Gourmet*, Alive Books.

Karen Knowler, founder of the UK organisation The Fresh Network, (www.fresh-network.com).

Chefs: Juliano (www.planetraw.com) and Chad Sarno (www.chadsarno.com) for their workshops and books.

THE DIFFERENCE A BIT OF
PASSION HAS MADE TO MY LIFE:

My passion for raw foods has transformed me personally and professionally. In both areas it has given me more joy and freedom than I had previously thought possible. Before I went raw I thought it was normal to have low energy, get flu three times a year and always have to work fixed hours for someone else. Following my passion taught me to think differently about food, and then think differently about every other area of my life. It has brought me many positive experiences and opportunities and has showed me that anything is possible.

Contact me on diana@rawsuperfoods.com

Take a look at my website: www.rawsuperfoods.com

JIM WHEAT

Jim Wheat is an Englishman in Dubai. The ex-marketing executive had climbed the corporate ladder but became disillusioned with the view. Quitting the rat race, he went travelling with his girlfriend Emma. They returned to Dubai nine months later as man and wife, following a Macchu Picchu proposal and barefoot wedding on Koh Samui, to live their passion.

ME AND MY PASSIONS:

I am passionate about encouraging people to discover their genius, become the best that they can and to dispense enthusiasm and support at every opportunity. I thrive on inspiring people to contribute where they previously feared to tread.

ABOUT MY CAREER:

My career these days entails combining my coaching and marketing background in a natural way to encourage colleagues and affiliates to find their own genius through authentic communication. Some organisations are fraught with politics, bad vibes and plain old fed up people. My aim is to rectify this. I offer corporates and the people within them the chance to make a difference by, for example, living by their own belief system and their brand. Many company charters and visions are just words on the wall and not often lived by – and how can they be when they are so impersonal? From CEO through to receptionist, everyone in an organisation plays a valid and valued part. I come in to help employees really understand how important their contribution is and that their part is adding up to a very great whole.

In my spare time, I am an executive coach and thrive on helping can-do individuals create their legacy through vision-setting and motivating them to realise their often untapped potential.

HOW I FOUND MY PASSION:

I found my passion when I learnt to accept that quiet times alone are not a bad thing. This much-needed 'vitamin me' opened my mind to reading and ultimately expressing my thoughts in written medium. It forced me to picture the day of my funeral, work back from there and decide what was important to me and how I could create a legacy. At the time, with a Masters degree in Civil Engineering in my back pocket, I had bounced up the career ladder with spells as a consultant, contractor, salesman and marketeer, obtaining relevant qualifications along the way. I realised that unless I changed my day-to-day 'reason to be' I'd equate to making little difference bar improving my typing skills on email.

The only thing that came in the way of me starting to work with my passions was my ingrained conditioning to conform and climb the corporate ladder. I decided to leave the corporate world behind and start my own company, Pure Originals, which has the tagline 'passionately unique' and which is all about being true to yourself, giving your own unique contribution. In addition it means that we are unique in everything we do. Practically, this came about following seven months demonstrating my 'brand magic' to three or four clients and holding workshops on vision, mission and values. One client in particular asked me to get involved with them longer term . . .

"It's great you talk the talk, Jim," he said, "but what about walking it?"

With this particular client I conducted workshops with not only senior management but also with its Hindu labourers. It was their input that was the most profound regarding their reasons and motivation for going to work and their vision. I went on to form their company charter, based on the group feedback and am now practising what I preach at the company and have 135 keen men to inspire. I've just finalised upgrading a labour camp based on the premise that all office staff should be comfortable eating the same dhaal that the labourers eat – me included! It's as far removed from the corporate world I knew as I could have imagined.

HOW I MADE MY PASSION MY REALITY:

To begin with I designed a questionnaire that asked my clients why they thought the company was in business in the first place, what their vision was and how they were contributing to making that happen. Living in Dubai, I have seen some amazing results with the most inspiring answers coming from that Hindi labourer and a Filipino receptionist – people who would never normally be given a voice – one that is rarely heard and sadly disregarded.

Practically, I realised my passion by following these six steps:

- Step 1: Quiet time visualising the future.
- Step 2: Resigning from work.
- Step 3: Selling stuff, quitting the pension scheme and emptying my rainy day fund.
- Step 4: Taking time out and travelling with my soulmate.
- Step 5: Working on a cause, not just a business.

- Step 6: Learning by the seat of my pants every day.

WHO HELPED ME ALONG THE WAY:

- Tom Peters, Re-Imagine, Dorling Kindersley Publishers Ltd.
- Spencer Johnson, The Present: The Gift that makes you Happy and Successful at Work and in Life, Bantam.
- Mark Forstater, The Living Wisdom of Socrates: Ancient Philosphy for Modern Wisdom, Coronet.
- Malcolm Gladwell, The Tipping Point, Abacus.
- David Baum, Lightening in a Bottle, Kaplan Business.
- Robin Sharma, The Monk who Sold his Ferrari, Element Books.
- R.L Wing, The Tao of Power (IChing), Bantam Doubleday Dell Publishing Group.
- Rolf Jensen, The Dream Society, McGraw-Hill Education.
- Patricia Schultz, 1,000 Places to see Before you Die, Workman Publishing.

THE DIFFERENCE A BIT OF
PASSION HAS MADE TO MY LIFE:

Now I can walk into a room and proudly hand over my business card as an extension of my being. Before, I felt like a fraud and handing over the business card was just to remind people of my status. Then I was 100 kg in weight, now I'm 84 kg. My previous hobbies were really just outlets for my aggression: in the gym or hurting someone on the rugby or football pitch.

Now my passion in my work takes away the need to have this testosterone outlet. I'm striving to be a 'gentle-man' and would like to be remembered that way. Labels and stereotyping have fallen away and as the labels fall, I become more genuine, more authentic and more me. Now I help others do the same. Liberation from the confines of corporate life have left me with more energy and optimism.

Contact me through:
www.gosmelltheflowers.com/blog

Take a look at my website:
www.gosmelltheflowers.com

ANDY LOPATA

 *Andy Lopata is recognised as one of the leading experts on business networking. Eight years ago, he joined Business Referral Exchange on a temporary basis, and later took on the role of Managing Director of what went on to become one of the UK's best respected networks. This proved to be a real door-opener. He is also co-author of Building a Business on Bacon and Eggs and the Amazon bestseller ...And Death Came Third!*

ME AND MY PASSIONS:

I have a passion for networking and like to share what I know by writing and speaking about how to do it effectively.

Eight years ago I started working for a company called Business Referral Exchange (BRE), which specialises in creating and managing business breakfast clubs all over the UK. The breakfast club's purpose is to facilitate networking and thus create business for its members on a referral basis. Back then I had never heard of networking, although I was busy speaking to people, getting to know people and connecting people all of the time. I just hadn't put a label on it. It soon became my passion. It hadn't always been that way.

Towards the end of 2003, I was surprised when, within a fortnight of each other, I received the same feedback from two speaking colleagues whom I respect very highly. Both of them told me, having seen me give the same talk, that I lacked any passion. After my initial disappointment, I took their feedback and went back to the drawing board. I looked at what I spoke about and asked myself how I felt about it. I tried to discover when I was at my most enthusiastic and when I was, perhaps, just going through the motions.

A lot of people say that they like hearing speakers talk about their own experiences. So I started working out what had happened to me that could illustrate the points I was trying to make. And what did I most enjoy talking about?

At the time I had two main presentations that I gave called 'The Art of Networking' and 'Winning with Champions'. Having reworked both of them, I soon rediscovered the spring in my step. A few months later I had to give a 'showcase' presentation to a group of professional speakers. They would be asked to feedback to me what they liked and what they felt could be improved about my talk. I was determined to make the latter extremely difficult for them, and ensure that no one could fault my passion! When I gave the talk my whole body was buzzing. It felt like a surge of electricity was pulsing through my veins. I suppose that I was in 'the zone'. Speaker after speaker came up and talked about how passionate I had been and how much I obviously believed in what I was speaking about. And they all said that they had struggled to find anything to critique.

I still have two key presentations, but they are nothing like the two I had back then. And no two presentations are ever alike. I am always coming up with new ideas and stories to incorporate, sometimes during the week, sometimes in the car and sometimes during the talk itself. I even find myself dreaming of new ideas and rushing to my computer in the middle of the night to write them down!

And, since the end of 2003, no-one has ever suggested to me that my talks lack passion.

ABOUT MY CAREER:

When I started with BRE it was on a part-time basis. It was a family-run business and I was brought in to cold call and help build a new business while I started building up my own career as a freelance writer. Suffice to say, the writing plans were soon shelved, although ironically I have now written about networking and referral strategy in several publications and had two books published on the topic, *Building a Business on Bacon and Eggs* and the Amazon bestseller *...And Death Came Third!*

BRE was the company that really got my career in networking moving. These days I take that knowledge into bigger organisations and help them look at how their staff and teams interact and how they use networking to build relationships with their prospects, customers and suppliers.

After becoming more involved with BRE, I was asked to give various presentations about networking. It was after I joined the Professional Speakers Association (www.professionalspeakers.org) that I really came into my own. Learning the techniques of leading speakers encouraged me to develop my own presentations and to write more. I began to understand more and more about networking and to develop my own ideas. I built an eight-week training programme, which took networking skills to a new level and have improved this further and further over subsequent years.

Each time I have a new idea about how to improve networking, I feel passionate about sharing it with as many people as possible, and really helping companies put it into action. It frustrates me to see big companies

133

focused more on sales training than networking and referral training for their teams and that still too many business people fail to see the value of networking for their own and their company's success.

HOW I MADE MY PASSION MY REALITY:

After a number of jobs in the eight years after leaving university, I quit my job with an American corporate to work for myself as a freelance writer. Six months earlier my father had started a new business, BRE, with a partner and they invited me to join them to help out, so that I could earn some money while I won some writing contracts. Although I am no longer with BRE, the rest, as they say, is history.

I WAS HELPED ALONG THE WAY BY:

The Professional Speakers Association, (www.professionalspeakers.org).

Jung Chang, *Wild Swans*, HarperPerennial.

Mike Southon and Chris West, *Beermat Entrepreneur*, Prentice Hall.

Tracy Plaice, *Face the Music and Win!*, Brave Press.

Bob Burg, *Endless Referrals*, McGraw-Hill Education.

James Surowiecki, *Wisdom of Crowds*, Abacus.

Richard McCann, *Just a Boy*, Ebury Press.

Julie Wright and Russ King, *We All Fall Down*, North River Press.

Paul Rusesabagina, *An Ordinary Man*, Viking Books.

Charlie Connelly, *Many Miles*, Charlton Athletic Football Club.

Bill Gates, *The Road Ahead,* Longman; N.e.of Abridged Ed edition.

THE DIFFERENCE A BIT OF
PASSION HAS MADE TO MY LIFE:

I am amazed by the amount I have developed since joining BRE and I wouldn't recognise the person who entered this industry. I frequently comment on how much I have learnt in this time compared to all previous learning, whether formal or otherwise. The opportunities open to me now are far in excess of anything I could ever have dreamed of.

Contact me on andy@lopata.co.uk

Take a look at my website: www.lopata.co.uk

DEBBIE JENKINS

Following a 'Perfect Day' session, Debbie Jenkins set up a best-selling publishing business, BookShaker.com, and moved from Birmingham to Spain with her husband Marcus in 2005.

ME AND MY PASSIONS:

I have a passion for matchmaking and turning ideas into wealth. Publishing is like alchemy and the whole idea that you can create money out of thin air is exciting! In the case of BookShaker.com I get to match experts with readers hungry for their knowledge, while ensuring I have a business that supports me in the life I want to live. By sharing profit and effort 50:50 with authors we can create an "evolutionarily stable equilibrium" for our business and life which, if adopted by us all, would lead to far more happiness in the world.

ABOUT MY CAREER:

I run BookShaker.com, an online publishing company, which means I can run the business from wherever in the world I choose to be. I have only actually met a handful of our authors face-to-face; we do most of our contact via email and Skype, and sell their books through traditional outlets and the internet. Since finding our passion we've succeeded in publishing 33 books in just under two years, achieving five bestsellers so far and enjoying our new homes and less hectic lifestyles.

Taking my love for publishing books even further, we have plans to create the world's first range of travel guides written by the readers for the readers. We call this process Bookworking™ and you can see it in action at NativeSpain (www.NativeSpain.com)

HOW I FOUND MY PASSION:

I spent years training as an electronics engineer and went on to work for several companies including British Telecom and a seedy slot machine company. Although this had led to a reasonable level of 'financial success', sitting in front of a computer screen in a windowless office drawing pictures of circuit-boards for 40 plus hours of my life a week was making me miserable. So, when I was headhunted by a manufacturing recruitment consultancy I jumped at the chance for a change and soon found I had a knack for matchmaking, creating win-wins and making money in the process. Of course, as a child, I never ever thought, "I want to be a recruitment consultant when I grow up." And so after a few years as the company's top fee earner I was yearning to sack my boss and go it alone – but not in recruitment.

At the time, the world wide web was just starting to be taken seriously and my, then out-of-work, graphic designer brother, Joe, had developed a knack for creating websites. So, putting my matchmaking skills into practice again, I convinced my boss to have a company website designed by my brother.

The increase in business my boss achieved as a result and the amount of money my brother earned for a relatively small amount of his time (£2,500) stirred my entrepreneurial ambitions further although it was almost another year before I'd saved enough money to make the leap.

I got thinking with my husband Marcus about the perfect online marketing business. I called Joe who was then working for an ad agency in Birmingham to see if he'd go into business with me. He agreed and so I left work.

For the first three months of our business Joe carried on in his job and would pop to my house at weekends, evenings and on his lunch break to design our business cards, website and letterheads. I'd spend every day tapping contacts and calling people up to see if I could sell them on the idea of using a website – it worked and once we had enough contracts to keep us going my brother could finally hand in his notice too and work on the business full time.

But after a while we became unhappy. We didn't want to admit it but we'd created a business that enslaved us, not a business we loved. Rather than give up we kept plodding on – but without the same passion that had got us to where we were and things began to fall apart. Out of necessity we made lots of our staff redundant, dumped the large offices and started rebuilding ourselves and the business the way we needed to. We wrote our first book *The Gorillas Want Bananas*. The acclaim it got us kept us in business and made us a nice profit again but we were still stuck as a service business, swapping our time for money.

This was a challenge – we knew that if we had traditional clients, in a service business (which was what we had started out doing) then we would never be able to escape – we would always be needed by them.

After a while operating in 'survival mode' we sat down and decided what a Perfect Day would look like. What we'd be doing. Where we'd be living. Who we'd be with. How we'd be spending our time. This Perfect Day session gave us the spark we needed to reinvent ourselves, use the skills we'd developed and have a lot more fun. We set out to get paid multiple times for a single effort and spend the rest of our time doing fun and exciting stuff and Bookshaker (www.BookShaker.com) was born.

As well as giving us really exciting things to aim for the Perfect Day exercise made us realise that we didn't want clients to pay us – we wanted to pay them! We wanted to be able to *send* money to the people we loved working with. We wanted to be writing *them* cheques instead of chasing them for payment! We wanted to take their knowledge and sell it for them to people who would benefit hugely from the advice in the books they bought.

I was doing matchmaking again and this time everyone would win!

HOW I MADE MY PASSION MY REALITY:

In order to break away from the old model of selling our time we had to take a drastic step. We stopped taking on paying clients which ate straight into our income. But it freed up our time and gave us back the buzz we had from starting our first business. This meant giving ourselves massive pay cuts and investing everything back into the publishing business.

We knew by breaking away from the traditional 'paid for' service, to a paid on results service we would be able to free up our most valuable asset, our time. Plus using the technology provided by print on demand and the internet we could also run the business from anywhere in the world. And it worked!

Within a few months Joe was able to get out of Birmingham and move to the Norfolk coast – one of his Perfect Day "must-haves". The proof this provided, that we could still run a thriving business while physically located apart, led me to finalise the plans for my own move. In September 2005 my husband and I moved to Spain – to a cave house in the mountains.

I WAS HELPED ALONG THE WAY BY:

I'm not very good at asking for help, so most of the things I've learned have been from reading books and modelling the success of others in all fields of life and business.

The most influential books have been:

Michael E. Gerber, *The E-Myth Revisited*, HarperCollins.

Mark Victor Hansen and Robert Allen, *One Minute Millionaire*, Vermilion.

Robert T. Kiyosaki, *Rich Dad, Poor Dad*, Time Warner Paperbacks.

Also, Jo Parfitt's 'Release The Book Within' course gave me the courage and skills to get that first book in print.

My husband Marcus has definitely been a stabilising and inspirational influence too and has always encouraged me and supported me to follow things I'm passionate about.

THE DIFFERENCE A BIT OF PASSION HAS MADE TO MY LIFE:

Since finding my passion, I've completely transformed physically, emotionally and mentally. Over the last ten years I have become someone I wouldn't have recognised and during the last two in particular, I have changed totally. I'm no longer such a control freak, I'm much more relaxed and easy going and more outward focused and less inclined to worry about the little things.

Take a look at our websites: www.BookShaker.com and www.NativeSpain.com

JOEL ARMSDEN

Joel Armsden is the creator of eARmusic, a brand new concept in what is known as 'artist and repertoire' or A&R, which he hopes will re-shape the way music is owned and distributed.

ME AND MY PASSIONS:

Discovering new music, discovering nice people in the music industry, sticking together with them and hopefully helping new artists to develop and find new ways of distributing their music on terms better suited to them. I love the thought of re-shaping the way in which music is owned and distributed.

ABOUT MY CAREER:

I am the creator of eARmusic, a new concept of A&R where new music is brought to the attention of industry bodies externally, through the web. It's e-A&R, hence eARmusic! To gain exposure for young, unsigned bands, I run a couple of showcase gigs, three open-mic nights (when artists can just turn up and play) and the odd feature night at a larger venue every week in London, where I'll book a signed and buzzing band to get the public in and fill the support slots with eARmusic artists.

I've also invested in some live and studio recording equipment and now run a live EP and demo-recording service for those who don't want to pay for a week in a studio. I have a new website, which is currently under development and which will encourage users to interact within the site and hopefully develop our online community, whilst 2007 will also see our first official music release – a band called Inbetween Days.

HOW I FOUND MY PASSION:

Like so many people, I've always loved music – I've always wanted to be the first to find the new band to listen to. I love soundtracks to films and always took on the task of video editing at university so I could lay down my own. Come dissertation time, I wanted to find a topic that interested me so I opened a load of music industry books, which is where I learned about the concept of A&R. That was definitely the first time I'd set my sights on a career.

So then, after Uni, armed with a bar job and having started my first regular gig night, I took up any work experience I could get. The experience included going into record label companies, booking agents and any other businesses related to music where I'd run odd jobs and more importantly, make contacts. It was then that I began to realise that the majority of jobs in the music industry were simply office jobs and that the role of the A&R man had changed somewhat from that which I had previously read about – in my opinion for the worse. This made me question whether I really wanted to work for a record label and I began to realise that actually getting out there and promoting live and unsigned music was far closer to what I wanted to be doing.

I always felt pretty lucky that my parents never pushed me into 'getting a proper job' during the first couple of years when I was working for free for any record label or music industry body that would take me!

Perhaps it all started to pay off when I booked a band for a gig, just before they started to 'buzz' in the industry. As luck would have it, I had work experience lined up at a number of major labels the week after and a massive bidding war ensued as I brought the band to their attention. Although in the end they signed to a label that I had nothing to do with – undoubtedly they'd have gone on to do what they're doing today regardless of my involvement – I figured a few priceless seeds had been sewn.

HOW I MADE MY PASSION MY REALITY:

I went travelling straight after Uni but having learnt about A&R through my dissertation, my plan was always to move to London once I got back and to pursue my A&R goal.

I knew nobody in the city when I first moved there, which was pretty tough but it also meant that all my time and energy went towards the music industry. I had just one contact so I helped her in any way I could, whilst emailing every recruitment agency, record label, manager and publisher I could think of, grabbing hold of any opportunity that came my way.

I regularly found myself working for nothing, in departments of music companies that I had little or no interest in, though at that point, it was all about building contacts. Meanwhile I spent my evenings working in a bar so I could pay the bills. At one point I had four work-experience placements, a bar job to pay the bills and an Alan Partridge video for any time I had off!

Whilst sniffing around these elusive A&R departments and taking them any good artists who played at the open-mic night I'd started, it was becoming clear to me that A&R wasn't all that I had read about in the books. They were written last decade – before the internet. It was at this point that I decided to have a go on my own, leave the bar work and work experience and develop the open-mic nights. These first spread to a couple of bars and a showcase gig, and are now three open-mics and two showcases every single week.

I then developed the eAR Music website. I took a few bands to labels that went on to sign major deals, and who will hopefully carry the eARmusic name through the music industry with them!

WHO HELPED ME ON THE WAY:

My one initial contact who hooked me up with work experience at a few places really helped me get the ball rolling. However irrelevant the music companies were that I was working for, every person I met was another contact, who opened new doors.

The MD of a well-known funky house label was particularly helpful – he didn't so much open doors for me, but he did make me realise what I needed to improve on. I had some pretty awful work placements too, sometimes for people younger than me, but rather than letting this get me down, it helped me become more determined. In fact, the awful placements were probably my strongest motivating force!

And now I'm in regular contact with a former major-label head of A&R, who gives me his backing not only by connecting me with good contacts but he also pays me to do whatever work he can offer, such as making live recordings.

Publications that proved helpful include:

The Music Week Directory, Nick Tesco, CMP Information Limited.

Music Week (see http://www.musicweek.com for further details).

I would also recommend any music press that suits your specific tastes so that you know what's going on in the area that you want to get involved in.

Although with the music industry, I would honestly suggest that rather than referring to any specific publications and learning theories, it's much more about getting stuck in, head first and accepting that you'll be starting from the bottom. It's also important to try and talk to any role models.

THE DIFFERENCE A BIT OF
PASSION HAS MADE TO MY LIFE:

I didn't have a professional life before this so it's hard to say – this is all I know of work! I'm very happy to be doing what I like doing, as a job, although there are things that I'd like to change. As it's my company I love working on developing it, though it doesn't leave much time for a social life unless I put up definite boundaries as to what is work time and what is play time. Working from a desk at the end of my bed isn't much fun after a while. Sometimes I forget to leave the house!

Working with my passion every day feels awesome, though! I have been massively inspired by the enjoyment of putting on a successful gig and finding music that is unknown. There is something to be said about working too closely to your passion and perhaps that can take an element of enjoyment out of it sometimes. It can also be frustrating to see musicians you respect and appreciate go un-noticed, while others who are more far more predictable and less creative go on to sign huge record deals and have money poured into them by labels. Aside from that, it's great if you can help someone who's creating something that you love too.

Contact me on: joel@earmusic.co.uk

Take a look at my website: www.earmusic.co.uk

STEPHANIE WARD

Stephanie Ward has always had a knack for business. With a business and marketing background, she has always understood what makes businesses tick. These days she puts those skills to use in her own venture, Firefly Coaching, where she helps small business owners grow their businesses into long-term sustainable enterprises.

ME AND MY PASSIONS:

My passion is helping small business owners grow their businesses into long-term sustainable enterprises and have a great life at the same time.

ABOUT MY CAREER:

I combine my business and marketing background, my coaching skills and my own personal experiences to live out my passion for helping people to grow successful businesses that are in line with their personal goals. As a business owner myself I understand what my clients are going through. I attract clients who are entrepreneurial thinkers, creative, and willing to do what is needed to reach their goals. I believe each unique person has special gifts that they are meant to use and by doing so, create happiness and joy for themselves and the people they serve.

How I found my passion:

I had been searching for my passion, at various levels of intensity, since I completed my undergraduate business degree. After working in my first job for several years it was time for a change and I went back to university and got my Master's degree in communication.

Following graduate school, I found a new job at a company I was passionate about and enjoyed working there for many years. I had the opportunity to work in several positions including business development, sales, marketing, and management and I also got to work in diverse locations. I had to leave that company when I decided to move to the Netherlands in 1999.

The next jobs I had were less fulfilling and lacked meaning, leading to a more urgent need to find my passion. I had tried to figure out what I wanted to do on my own by reading books, doing exercises and talking to people. I was putting in a lot of effort but wasn't really getting anywhere. I finally reached a point of total frustration and thought, "well, at least I'm very clear about the things I *don't* want." So, I started writing a description of all of the things I didn't want anymore, like an extremely long commute and work that didn't feel like the best use of my time and energy. Through that, some of the things I did want became more evident, although I still didn't have the answer.

I decided that if I couldn't discover my passion on my own, I would find someone to help me. I sent that description to three people. One of them, an author and the owner of a coaching company, answered immediately. At the time I wasn't really familiar with the concept of coaching and had heard about it for the first time in her book. Through that, I felt that working with a coach could help me. So I hired one of her coaches, who specialised in helping people find their passion. By working with her, I realised that I wanted to be a coach myself! I had finally found a profession and a way to help people that felt perfect.

HOW I MADE MY PASSION MY REALITY:

Once I knew that coaching was right for me, I enrolled in a coach-training programme, which I completed during the evening over two years while working full-time. After graduating from the course, I started my own coaching business in April 2004. I had a website designed, joined some networking groups, and started to get the word out about my new business. I've learned a lot since then about how to start your own business and attract clients and now I share everything I know with my clients to help them grow their own businesses.

Another key ingredient has been determination and persistence. Everyone has bad days and the secret is to keep going in spite of them. Staying connected to the vision you have about your business will get you through the hard times and inspire you to continuously move forward.

WHO HELPED ME ON THE WAY:

A healthy support system is essential to a happy and prosperous life. You don't have to do it all alone, and it is smart to ask for help. Practically, I have been helped by:

Byron Katie, *Loving What Is*, Rider & Co.

Eckhart Tolle, *The Power of Now*, Hodder & Stoughton Ltd.

Robert Kiyosaki, *Rich Dad, Poor Dad*, Time Warner Paperbacks.

Miguel Ruiz, *The Four Agreements*, Universe Publishing.

Lynn Grabhorn, *Excuse Me, Your Life is Waiting*, Hodder Mobius.

Tim Sanders, *Love is the Killer App*, Three Rivers Press.

THE DIFFERENCE A BIT OF PASSION HAS MADE TO MY LIFE:

Being able to do work that I am passionate about, helping people, and making a living doing it is the most amazing gift of my life. I have never been happier and am so grateful to be able to spend my energy in a way that is meaningful to me. Life is short and it goes by quickly, much too fast to spend it doing something that isn't authentically you.

Contact me on: stephanie@fireflycoaching.com

If you are a Business Owner who would like to attract more clients, then take a look at my website: www.fireflycoaching.com and grab your free copy of my special report, *7 Steps to Attract More Clients in Less Time* plus free monthly business building tips.

MICHAEL CHISSICK

Michael Chissick is the creator of YogaBuds, a pioneering concept in children's yoga. He is the first man in the UK to succeed in getting yoga onto the school curriculum as a means of improving children's self-esteem. Consequently he created an Edexcel-accredited training programme to enable him to train others to be able to do the same throughout the UK.

ME AND MY PASSIONS:

Seeing children successfully increase their self-esteem, concentration and capacity to learn through yoga.

ABOUT MY CAREER:

I am a qualified yoga teacher and have now succeeded in getting yoga onto the national curriculum. There is a special emphasis on bringing yoga to children with special needs and especially those who suffer attention deficit disorders. The effect of yoga on these children allows them to relax and concentrate for longer periods of time.

My work is divided up into three main areas: teaching yoga to children in both mainstream and special schools and then teaching the adults who will teach them.

In Primary Schools I teach the whole class, which means that everyone including children with mild and severe learning difficulties are included. If it weren't for this I am convinced that the children who most needed the class would not turn up.

My approach focuses on improving children's confidence, self esteem, communication skills social skills and challenging behaviour. I have been remarkably successful in teaching children skills and techniques that enable them to relax and self calm, for example in situations where anger could be king.

I achieve my goals by ensuring the yoga is achievable by everyone, by making the posture work fun through games, activities and sometimes stories that children can relate to.

I also teach in Special Needs Schools and here I am more focused on improving communication and sense of achievement through the yoga. The challenges here are far greater, of course, but over the last seven years I have developed and continue to develop strategies to help meet them.

Teaching adults the BTEC Advanced Diploma for Teaching Yoga to Children enables me to spread the reach of what I do to the whole of the UK.

How I found my passion:

In 1990 my wife Jill died suddenly. My children Andrew and Claire were eight and twelve respectively. I was running my own business as a paper merchant at the time but sold the business in order to bring up my children. As a result I needed something to do that allowed me to look after them and ended up joining a course called 'Access to BEd Primary', although I knew little about Access courses. In fact, rather naively, it would be fair to say, I had no idea what it meant.

People kept saying that I would make a good teacher but I was perplexed as to why they might say that. Finally it dawned on me that I was heading to a Bachelor's of Education – ah so that was what BEd stood for! I would become a qualified primary school teacher. My naïvety was astounding, admittedly and I found myself surprised but very enthusiastic. During the course, I became very interested in self-esteem and in particular, in ways of enhancing children's self-esteem.

I began practising yoga in 1974. When I was training to become a qualified yoga teacher, I could see that I could use my skills and experiences as a primary school teacher to teach yoga to children in such a way that their self-esteem would be improved. I began teaching children as an after-school activity but soon realised that it would be more effective if it took place during curriculum time.

It wasn't long before all the signs were there that I was on the right track. Children were telling me how much they enjoyed the lessons, that they were practising at home and even teaching the rest of the family. When 'Lydia' stood in 'stick poster' without holding on to her walking frame and 'Stevie' showed his (SEN) class how well he could do 'candle posture' I knew I was 'home'.

HOW I MADE MY PASSION MY REALITY:

In 1999 I set up YogaBuds and began to teach yoga to special needs children at Phoenix School, which is in Bow in East London. This was (and still is) pioneering work. The Telegraph Magazine published an article about what I was doing, which provoked great interest across the country and led to more work in primary schools. By this time my reputation was spreading and demand was outstripping my ability to supply, so I decided to write a training programme based on my experiences in order to create and train more YogaBuds teachers. The training course was eventually accredited by Edexcel, which is a leading force in educational and vocational accreditation. Soon after, learners were signing up for the very first course, *The Advanced Diploma for Teaching Yoga to Children.*

The second cohort is now well under way and YogaBuds teachers are now teaching in schools around the country.

WHO HELPED ME ON THE WAY:

Bob Insley encouraged me to become a qualified yoga teacher and is the most inspirational adult yoga teacher I have met in 35 years of yoga.

Petra Prossowsky, the best children's yoga teacher in Germany and my co-author of *Moving Stories*, a children's yoga book.

Veronica Armson gave me my first break by asking me to come into her school to teach yoga to children with learning difficulties including ASD, ADHD, and EBD.

My son Andrew has encouraged me through difficult and good times, reminding me of the importance of the work and the efficacy of my teaching skills.

Jenny Mosely, LDA, *Quality Circle Time in the Primary Classroom*, LDA.

H Jerome Freiberg Merrill, *Freedom to Learn*, Carl Rogers, Merrill.

Denis Lawrence, Paul Chapman, *Enhancing Self Esteem in the Classroom*, Bantam.

Carla Hannaford, *Smart Moves*, Great Ocean.

Stella Weller, *Yoga for Children*, Thorsons.

Mary Stewart, Kathy Phillips, *Yoga for Children*, Simon & Schuster.

Thia Luby, *Children's Book of Yoga*, Clear Light.

THE DIFFERENCE A BIT OF PASSION HAS MADE TO MY LIFE:

I now have the reputation of being one of the top teachers in Europe. I'm invited to give lectures in Germany and the UK. I have written a book called *Moving*

Stories, which is doing very well in Germany and I am writing a new book called *How to Teach Yoga to Children in School.* I have improved my skills of training people and I feel very proud of myself. I love doing what I do and am doing what I am passionate about.

Contact me on: info@yogabuds.org.uk

Take a look at my website: www.yogabuds.org.uk

ABOUT THE AUTHOR

Jo Parfitt is passionate about words and it is because of this that she has become a writer, journalist, speaker, teacher, trainer, author, publisher and publishing consultant.

Since having her first book accepted by the first publisher she approached back in 1985, she has gone on to have over 20 books published on subjects ranging from computers, through careers, to cookery. In 1987 she married an 'oil and gas man' and began a life as an expat wife. It took a few years, but over time she realised she had become passionate about living and working overseas too.

It was only natural that she began to incorporate everything she had learned and her passions into her work. In 1996 Jo formed Summertime Publishing, which is best known for her handbook on the portable careers, called *A Career in Your Suitcase* and went on to publish many more books on life abroad.

More recently, Lean Marketing Press (www.bookshaker.com) have published *Expat Entrepreneur* and *Expat Writer - Release the Book Within*. Once editor of the international magazine, *Woman Abroad*, she has seen hundreds of her articles published all over the world for magazines, broadsheets and websites. Key 'Jo Parfitt' into Google or some other search engine for proof that she is a prolific and versatile writer.

For the past six years Jo has focused on sharing her knowledge. She runs classes called *Release the Book Within, Definite Articles, The Expat Writer, The Expat Entrepreneur, A Career in Your Suitcase* and *Find Your Passion*, which are all available as both workshops and books. With the aid of a team of trusted, similarly published, associates, Jo also offers a full editing and publishing consultancy service called The Book Cooks to those eager to see their name in print.

Jo is happily married to Ian, and together with their boys, Sam and Josh, they have lived in Dubai, Oman, Norway, England and now the Netherlands.

Find out more about her work at her websites

The Book Cooks
www.thebookcooks.com

Career in Your Suitcase
www.career-in-your-suitcase.com

Expat Entrepreneur
www.expatentrepreneurs.com

Summertime Publishing
www.summertimepublishing.com

RESOURCES

BOOKS

Jo Parfitt, *Career in Your Suitcase 2*, Summertime Publishing

Jo Parfitt and Jacqui Tillyard, *Grow Your Own Networks*, Summertime Publishing

Jo Parfitt, *So, You Want to Write a Book*, Summertime Publishing

Jo Parfitt, *Expat Entrepreneur*, Lean Marketing Press

Jo Parfitt, *The Expat Writer - Release the Book Within*, Lean Marketing Press

Arvind Devalia, *Get the Life you Love*, Nirvana Publishing

John Clark, *Your Money or Your Life*, Century

Dr Katherine Benziger, *Thriving in Mind*, (www.benziger.org)

Barbara Sher, *I Could Do Anything I Wanted if Only I Knew What it Was*, Hodder and Stoughton

Nathalie Goldberg, *Writing Down the Bones*, Shambala

Julia Cameron, *The Artist's Way*, Pan Macmillan

Nancy Anderson, *Work with Passion*, New World Library

Ros Taylor, *Transform Yourself*, Kogan Page

Marsha Sinetar, *Do What You Love and The Money Follows*, Dell Trade Paperback

Richard Bolles, *What Color is Your Parachute?* Ten Speed Press

Dr Phil McGraw, *Life Strategies*, Vermilion

Dr Phil McGraw, *Self Matters*, Simon and Schuster

Carmel McConnell, *Soultrader*, Momentum

Sally Longman, *Choosing a Career*, The Times with Kogan Page

Gary Pyke and Stuart Neath, *Be Your Own Careers Consultant*, Momentum

Nick Williams, *The Work We Were Born to Do*, Element Books

PEOPLE

People and organisations who are passionate about passion:

The Book Cooks, a complete menu of publishing services from brainwave to bookshelf www.thebookcooks.com

Donna Messer, www.connectuscanada.com, www.businesstree.com, www.businesswomancanada.com

Dr Katherine Benziger, Developer of the BTSI indicator offers an assessment at (www.benziger.org)

Helen Eriksen, Going-Beyond (www.going-beyond.dk)

Jacinta Noonan, Soulworks (www.soulworks.nl), (www.bigontheinside.com)

Fiona Cowan, The Village Wordsmith, (www.fifix.com)

Jacqui Tillyard (www.jacquitillyard.com)

Val Plummer, Forever Living (www.forever-living.com)

Dave Scarlett, The Soul Millionaire (www.thesoulmillionaire.com)

Debbie Jenkins, www.leanmarketing.co.uk, www.bookshaker.com

Native Spain (www.nativespain.com)

Lesley Fisher, Careers consultant and business coach
(www.metamorphosisconsulting.nl)

CONFERENCES

The Women's International Networking Conference (WIN),
(www.winconference.com)

Families in Global Transition (FIGT) (www.figt.org)

7 PRACTICAL STEPS TO ADD PASSION TO YOUR LIFE AND BUSINESS

by Trish Tucker (www.passion4juice.com)

1. Start from the heart!

Passion is in all of us. Look deep into your heart to the ideas and activities that inspire and motivate you. Also ask yourself which things in your life you want to change. Deep reflection can provide you with fresh insights and may take you on a new adventure.

2. Discover your passions!

Create a list of ideas, activities and passion pastimes that inspire you and make you FEEL fantastic. Identify what you want to do and work out how to do these activities more often.

Perhaps you will uncover forgotten passions!

3. Dare to dream BIG

Don't postpone your dreams – life is too short to be dissatisfied! Review your goals and clarify your purpose. Always write down your dreams in present tense and imagine they are already coming true.

4. Create your personal passion plan

Clarify which dreams you are going to turn into goals. Define your next steps. Make your goals SMARTer (that's Specific, Measurable, Action-based, Realistic and Timed.

5. Just do it!

Review your passion plan on a daily basis. Know what you need to do this week about your passion and do not postpone it. Seek out opportunities to live your passion.

6. Turn your passion into powerful performance!

Patience is passion tamed. Make your dreams happen by accepting change and making tough decisions.

Be careful not to burden yourself with too many promises.

7. Share your passion & inspire others!

Tell people about your passions, and share your success when your dreams come true.

expat writer

RELEASE THE BOOK WITHIN

Jo Parfitt

www.bookshaker.com

"One of the best books there is for expatriates who want a career adventure. This book is packed with examples, tips and, of course, lots of inspiration. Don't forget to pack it before you set off on your new life."
Robin Pascoe, www.expatexpert.com

EXPAT
ENTREPRENEUR

How To Create and Maintain Your Own
Portable Career Anywhere In The World

JO PARFITT

www.expatentrepreneurs.com

If you've enjoyed reading
Find Your Passion
and think the story of how
you found your passion would
make a great book then talk
to The Book Cooks and
let us help you to cook up
the recipe for a bestseller

www.**TheBookCooks**.com
http://thebookcooks.wordpress.com
email: kitchen@TheBookCooks.com

Printed in the United Kingdom
by Lightning Source UK Ltd.
119621UK00001B/55-72